Compression
& Encryption
Algorithms & Software

by D. James Benton

Foreword

This book covers various algorithms for compression and encryption, some of which overlap, serving both purposes simultaneously. We will discuss why one algorithm works better for one case and not another as well as how different implementations are superior or more robust. All of the algorithms and code are presented in the C programming language and all are available free online.

Free Software

All of the examples contained in this book,
(as well as a lot of free programs) are available at...

https://www.dudleybenton.altervista.org/software/index.html

Programming

All of the examples presented in this book are implemented in the C programming language. The code, spreadsheets, data files, and other material are arranged in folders within a single ZIP archive that can be freely downloaded at the address above.

Ralphie's Decoder Ring

The Enigma Machine

Table of Contents

Ctl	Dec	Hex	Char	Code	Dec	Hex	Char	Dec	Hex	Char	Dec	Hex	Char
^@	0	00		NUL	32	20	sp	64	40	@	96	60	`
^A	1	01	☺	SOH	33	21	!	65	41	A	97	61	a
^B	2	02	☻	STX	34	22	"	66	42	B	98	62	b
^C	3	03	♥	ETX	35	23	#	67	43	C	99	63	c
^D	4	04	♦	EOT	36	24	$	68	44	D	100	64	d
^E	5	05	♣	ENQ	37	25	%	69	45	E	101	65	e
^F	6	06	♠	ACK	38	26	&	70	46	F	102	66	f
^G	7	07	•	BEL	39	27	'	71	47	G	103	67	g
^H	8	08	◘	BS	40	28	(	72	48	H	104	68	h
^I	9	09	○	HT	41	29	)	73	49	I	105	69	i
^J	10	0A	◙	LF	42	2A	*	74	4A	J	106	6A	j
^K	11	0B	♂	VT	43	2B	+	75	4B	K	107	6B	k
^L	12	0C	♀	FF	44	2C	,	76	4C	L	108	6C	l
^M	13	0D	♪	CR	45	2D	-	77	4D	M	109	6D	m
^N	14	0E	♫	SO	46	2E	.	78	4E	N	110	6E	n
^O	15	0F	☼	SI	47	2F	/	79	4F	O	111	6F	o
^P	16	10	►	SLE	48	30	0	80	50	P	112	70	p
^Q	17	11	◄	CS1	49	31	1	81	51	Q	113	71	q
^R	18	12	↕	DC2	50	32	2	82	52	R	114	72	r
^S	19	13	‼	DC3	51	33	3	83	53	S	115	73	s
^T	20	14	¶	DC4	52	34	4	84	54	T	116	74	t
^U	21	15	§	NAK	53	35	5	85	55	U	117	75	u
^V	22	16	▬	SYN	54	36	6	86	56	V	118	76	v
^W	23	17	↨	ETB	55	37	7	87	57	W	119	77	w
^X	24	18	↑	CAN	56	38	8	88	58	X	120	78	x
^Y	25	19	↓	EM	57	39	9	89	59	Y	121	79	y
^Z	26	1A	→	SUB	58	3A	:	90	5A	Z	122	7A	z
^[	27	1B	←	ESC	59	3B	;	91	5B	[	123	7B	{
^\	28	1C	∟	FS	60	3C	<	92	5C	\	124	7C		
^]	29	1D	↔	GS	61	3D	=	93	5D	]	125	7D	}
^^	30	1E	▲	RS	62	3E	>	94	5E	^	126	7E	~
^_	31	1F	▼	US	63	3F	?	95	5F	_	127	7F	⌂ †

Dec	Hex	Char	Dec	Hex	Char	Dec	Hex	Char	Dec	Hex	Char
128	80	Ç	160	A0	á	192	C0	└	224	E0	α
129	81	ü	161	A1	í	193	C1	┴	225	E1	ß
130	82	é	162	A2	ó	194	C2	┬	226	E2	Γ
131	83	â	163	A3	ú	195	C3	├	227	E3	π
132	84	ä	164	A4	ñ	196	C4	─	228	E4	Σ
133	85	à	165	A5	Ñ	197	C5	┼	229	E5	σ
134	86	å	166	A6	ª	198	C6	╞	230	E6	µ
135	87	ç	167	A7	º	199	C7	╟	231	E7	τ
136	88	ê	168	A8	¿	200	C8	╚	232	E8	Φ
137	89	ë	169	A9	⌐	201	C9	╔	233	E9	Θ
138	8A	è	170	AA	¬	202	CA	╩	234	EA	Ω
139	8B	ï	171	AB	½	203	CB	╦	235	EB	δ
140	8C	î	172	AC	¼	204	CC	╠	236	EC	∞
141	8D	ì	173	AD	¡	205	CD	═	237	ED	φ
142	8E	Ä	174	AE	«	206	CE	╬	238	EE	ε
143	8F	Å	175	AF	»	207	CF	╧	239	EF	∩
144	90	É	176	B0	░	208	D0	╨	240	F0	≡
145	91	æ	177	B1	▒	209	D1	╤	241	F1	±
146	92	Æ	178	B2	▓	210	D2	╥	242	F2	≥
147	93	ô	179	B3	│	211	D3	╙	243	F3	≤
148	94	ö	180	B4	┤	212	D4	╘	244	F4	⌠
149	95	ò	181	B5	╡	213	D5	╒	245	F5	⌡
150	96	û	182	B6	╢	214	D6	╓	246	F6	÷
151	97	ù	183	B7	╖	215	D7	╫	247	F7	≈
152	98	ÿ	184	B8	╕	216	D8	╪	248	F8	°
153	99	Ö	185	B9	╣	217	D9	┘	249	F9	·
154	9A	Ü	186	BA	║	218	DA	┌	250	FA	·
155	9B	¢	187	BB	╗	219	DB	█	251	FB	√
156	9C	£	188	BC	╝	220	DC	▄	252	FC	ⁿ
157	9D	¥	189	BD	╜	221	DD	▌	253	FD	²
158	9E	₧	190	BE	╛	222	DE	▐	254	FE	■
159	9F	ƒ	191	BF	┐	223	DF	▀	255	FF	

Chapter 1. Introduction

As motivation and purpose vary, so do compression and encryption algorithms. In the early days of computers, storage space was a significant concern, but that is now rarely the case. Even download/upload time-to-transmit is becoming less of an issue. Now packaging convenience and/or security is the primary impetus for compression and privacy is the chief incentive for encryption. We will discuss compression and encryption separately, though these often overlap.

Preliminaries

In order to discuss these topics, several concepts must first be understood, including: signed and unsigned characters and integers (bytes and words), character sets, and technical file I/O terminology. The reader is directed elsewhere for these preliminaries, including these topics:

https://en.wikipedia.org/wiki/Byte

https://en.wikipedia.org/wiki/Integer_(computer_science)

https://en.wikipedia.org/wiki/C_file_input/output

With the increasingly ubiquitous presence of Microsoft® Word®, even on Apple® products, many users are unaware that there is such a thing as the ASCII character set, that it differs from the Windows® Latin-1 character subset that first appears when inserting a symbol into a document, and that it was not always this way—even for Microsoft®. At one time there was the "PC character set", which was different from the ASCII, but even this disappeared long ago. There is a table on page iv and more on the ASCII character set can be found at:

https://en.wikipedia.org/wiki/ASCII

The way Microsoft® Word® treats characters as decorated, font-specific, multi-national, colorful, etc. [what's next, flavored and aromatic?] has little to do with files and data, bits and bytes. Don't confuse the two. While this document was created in MSWord®, that's where the overlap of these topics ends.

Types of Algorithms

There are two decisions when considering compression and/or encryption algorithms in the digital world of files and data. The first of these is lossless or lossy and the second is generic or targeted. These two binary questions do not combine (2x2=4) to make four *practical* paths. The term *lossy* means that some part of the original information will be lost (i.e., unrecoverable) in the process. The term *lossless* means the opposite: no information is lost in the process. The term *targeted* in this context means that you know something about the data that you can take advantage of and design the process around this knowledge. A targeted algorithm will only work on one type of data (or perhaps a very small group of data types). One might design a lossless algorithm for generic data or a lossless algorithm for targeted data or a lossy algorithm for targeted data, but it would be foolish to design a lossy algorithm for generic data.

The four most commonly encountered compression algorithms are associated with a specific file extension: GIF, JPG, MP3, and ZIP. GIF is a targeted lossless compression, designed to handle images having no more than 256 colors. JPG is targeted lossy compression, designed to handle 24-bit color or 8-bit black-and-white photographs. MP3 is a targeted lossy compression, designed to handle 8-bit or 16-bit mono or stereo audio files ZIP is lossless and generic.

Types of Data

Do not save a line drawing or chart or any image with sharp lines in a JPG, as this format is only suitable for photographs. Don't save a majestic mountain sunset or seaside sunrise as a GIF, or you will lose most of the hues. The WAV files you ripped from a CD are safe and secure as MP3s, because your ear can't tell the difference. ZIP works with any type of data, but much more efficient with some types than others. Why not save a line drawing or chart in a JPG? Because it will be blurry and you can never recover the original fine detail, as illustrated below:

We will also only be discussing data that can be or is typically stored and distributed in digital form. As for sensory perception data, we will only consider pictures, sounds, and combinations of the two (i.e., videos).

Chapter 2. Bits, Bytes, and Words

These basic data types are an artifact of computer hardware design. Intel® is currently the largest manufacturer of processors, but this was not always so. Intel® processors work with a variety of data element sizes, including: 8-bit (bytes or characters), 16-bit (words and short integers), 32-bit (integers and floats), 64-bit (long integers and floats), and 80-bit (integers and floats). Some IBM® mainframe computers used 64-bit and 128-bit integers and floats. CDC® built machines that used 60-bit integers and floats. Due to the prevalence of Intel® processors, computer users have become accustomed to thinking in terms of bytes.

Data Types and Bit Order

In this text we will be working in the context of Intel® and Windows®. The objects and terminology will presume this base of reference. A byte has 8 bits, a nibble is ½ byte or 4 bits, a signed short or unsigned word has 16 bits, a signed int or unsigned dword has 32 bits, a signed long or unsigned qword has 64 bits, a float has 32 bits, and a double has 64 bits.

We must also keep in mind the order in which bits are stored in memory and on the disk. Intel® processors are little endian and we will use this assumption throughout. The few remaining big endian machines will have to compensate accordingly. Test code can be found in folder examples\endian.

Compiling the Examples

All of the code samples and fully-functional example programs in this text have been written in the C language. There are no elements or features of C++ in any of the codes, as this is both unnecessary and inefficient. These have been compiled with the 32-bit Microsoft® C compiler and a batch file (_compile_something.bat) has been provided with each source code for convenience. All of the programs will compile with the 64-bit compiler without modification if you should need to do so, although this will have no appreciable impact on the performance.

I always compile code with the highest warning level (/W3) and treat warnings as errors (/WX) plus full optimization (/Ox) to identify unused variables. Code should compile with no warnings or errors whatsoever. Anything less demonstrates lack of attention to detail. Warnings and errors are generated for a reason and should not be ignored.

Frequency of Occurrence

The simplest and perhaps most common form of data is text. In the world of PCs, which follow the ASCII convention, the basic mode of storage for such data is one byte per character. We will start here and first consider the distribution of data. When it comes to text, some letters are used far more often than others, while some may never be used. In the English language, the letter "e" is used most often and "q" least, by a ratio of 56:1. After removing all the line breaks, letter count for the Gettysburg Address is listed below:

Gettysburg Address					
count	char	count	char	count	char
260	space	31	c	10	y
164	e	27	g	3	I
123	t	26	f	3	k
101	a	26	w	2	T
93	o	24	v	2	W
80	h	22	u	1	:
79	r	20	,	1	B
76	n	16	p	1	F
67	i	14	-	1	G
58	d	13	b	1	N
46	s	13	m	1	q
42	l	10	.		

Only 35 characters are used of the possible 256 (13.7%). If only 32 had been used, we could store the entire text in 5-bit data elements or 5 of the 8 bits, which make up a single byte. One type of compression is to simply remove the unnecessary bits. While this is inconvenient to work with in memory and files, it is possible and has been used. Some variant of this is used in all of the popular archiving utilities (WinZip, WinRAR, 7Zip, and tar).

It is interesting to note if 32 characters were sufficient and we simply used 5 out of 8 bits, this would require 62.5% of the bits even though we used only 12.5% of the possible characters. By this example we see that there is not a one-to-one correspondence between complexity and storage. If we needed only 65,536 words, these could all be represented by 16-bit unsigned integers so that any of those words could be represented by 2 bytes. Some compression algorithms are based on this concept. We might consider using 2 bits for some symbols, 3 bits for others, and so forth. This process is called *bit reduction*.

In order for bit reduction to be advantageous, the data must exhibit certain behavior, namely, there must be a disparity in the frequency of occurrence. If all values occurred with equal frequency, there would be no advantage representing any group of values differently from any other group. This disparity or lack thereof is often compared to distinct sounds vs. white noise. The spectrum (intensity vs. frequency) of a distinct sound exhibits a non-trivial pattern, while the spectrum of white noise is flat (the same intensity for all frequencies). See Appendix C for more on frequency of occurrence.

If we were to represent a group of data (in our case, a file) through some sort of bit reduction, taking advantage of the disparity of occurrence of the different possible values, and save this as a different group (again, a file), we might achieve some compression (i.e., the second file might be smaller than the first). The second file will necessarily not have the same disparity as the first. The implication is that this process cannot continue indefinitely. Eventually, the second file must be at least as large, if not larger than, the first. Were this not so, we could compress all information into nothing. Common sense confirms that this is not possible.

Examples

In the chapters that follow, we will first discuss various lossless compression methods, then lossy ones, and finally encryption. Examples will be provided in each section with functional source code and instructions for compilation and use. All of the examples, spreadsheets, and associated files can be found in the online archive in the examples folder. The archive can be freely downloaded at the address listed in the Forward.

Chapter 3. Shannon-Fano Trees

Shannon–Fano[1] coding is one of the earliest algorithms to take advantage of distribution disparity.[2] While not strictly optimal, this algorithm is illustrative and also of historical significance.[3] S-F trees can form the basis for lossless compression. We will begin our discussion of algorithms here.

The concept behind S-F trees is simple: count the characters and arrange them from most frequent to least. Split these into two sets, with as close to the same number in each set as possible. Split each of these sets in the same manner. Proceed until each set contains only a single character. S-F trees are built from the top down. One might think from this splitting process that the trees would roughly have the same number of levels as the power of 2 corresponding to the number of possibilities. This is true for equally-balanced branches, which is often not the case. For this reason, S-F is rarely used in practice; however, it is used in the IMPLODE compression method, which is part of the ZIP file format.[4]

We will use the following sentence to illustrate the process:

SHE SELLS SEA SHELLS BY THE SEA SHORE

The character count is listed in the following table, where b is for blank:

8	7	7	4	4	2	1	1	1	1	1
S	E	b	H	L	A	B	R	T	Y	O

The splits with count sums are as follows:

SEb=22	HLABRTYO=15
S=8	Eb=14
E=7	b=7
HL=8	ABRTYO=7
H=4	L=4
ABR=4	TYO=3
A=2	BR=2
B=1	R=1
TY=2	O=1
T=1	Y=1

The right branch has 5 splits or levels. There were only 11 unique characters, yet with a tree of depth 5, we could have represented $2^5=32$

---

[1] This algorithm is named after Claude Shannon and Robert Fano.

[2] Shannon, C. E., "A Mathematical Theory of Communication," Bell System Technical Journal, Vol. 27, pp. 379–423, 1948.

[3] Fano, R. M., "The Transmission of Information," MIT Technical Report No. 65., 1949.

[4] Details can be found on the PKWARE web site as well as Wikipedia.

possibilities. The final tree codes are listed in the following table, with 1 indicating the left branch and 0 indicating the right branch.

11	S
101	E
001	b
110	H
010	L
1100	A
10100	B
00100	R
11000	T
01000	Y
0000	O

The compressed data phrase requires a total of 115 bits, not including the table. This is an average of 3.11 bits per character. We see that $2^{3.11}$=8.62, which is less than 11 and much less than 32. Storing this string in ASCII requires 37*8=296 bits, making S-F a 61% reduction—again not counting the table, which is necessary to recover the original data.

In order to implement this algorithm, we must first read the input file, counting the characters, then build the tree, then store the tree in the output file, then rewind the input file, read through again, writing the codes to the output file, then close both files. The code (sfan.c) and files can be found in the examples\sfan folder.

Notice in the preceding table that we must keep track, not only of which branch (left or right/zero or one), but also how many branches for each code. With each split, we increment the number of bits for every member of the set, shift left one bit, and OR 1 on the left.. It's not necessary to OR 0 on the right. The tree splitting code is simple and reentrant:

```
void SplitTree(TREE*s,dword n)
  {
  dword i,j,k,l;
  if(n<2)
    return;
  i=0;
  j=s[i].n;
  k=n-1;
  l=s[k].n;
  while(k>i+1)
    if(j+s[i+1].n<=l+s[k-1].n)
      j+=s[++i].n;
    else
      l+=s[--k].n;
```

```
for(k=0;k<=i;k++)
   {
   s[k].l<<=1;
   s[k].l|=1;
   s[k].b++;
   }
for(k=i+1;k<n;k++)
   {
   s[k].l<<=1;
   s[k].b++;
   }
if(i)
   SplitTree(s,i+1);
if(n>i+2)
   SplitTree(s+i+1,n-i-1);
}
```

We must store the tree in the output file, as well as the length, and should also put some identifying code at the beginning.[5] This and subsequent example compression utilities are designed to be used as follows:

```
sfan option inputfilename outputfilename
```

In this case, option can be c for compress or e for expand. If upper case C/E is specified, the tree will also be listed. For the seashells text, we have...

```
C:\examples\sfan>sfan c seashells.txt seashells.sfa
Shannon-Fano tree compression utility
input file: seashells.txt
33 bytes input
11 unique characters
output file: seashells.sfa
40 bytes table
54 bytes output
-45.9% compression
```

The uncompressed input file is 33 bytes long and the compressed output file is 54 bytes long. The table alone requires 40 bytes. While this results in an expansion of 45.9% for this particular case, the algorithm does work. Next, we compress the Gettysburg Address...

```
C:\examples\sfan>sfan c GettysburgAddress.txt
   GettysburgAddress.sfa
Shannon-Fano tree compression utility
input file: GettysburgAddress.txt
1578 bytes input
52 unique characters
output file: GettysburgAddress.sfa
161 bytes table
```

---

[5] Windows® bitmap files begin with BM, Zip files begin with PK (for developer Phil Katz), PDFs begin with "%PDF", GIFs begin GIF89a, JPGs begin with JIFF, etc.

8

```
1047 bytes output
33.7% compression
```

Or perhaps the witches brew (Macbeth Act 4 Scene 1)...

```
C:\examples\sfan>sfan c WitchesBrew.txt WitchesBrew.sfa
Shannon-Fano tree compression utility
input file: WitchesBrew.txt
1302 bytes input
53 unique characters
output file: WitchesBrew.sfa
162 bytes table
938 bytes output
28.0% compression
```

Or the entire KJV Bible, including the Apocrypha:

```
C:\examples\sfan>sfan c KJV.txt KJV.sfa
Shannon-Fano tree compression utility
input file: KJV.txt
5436101 bytes input
86 unique characters
output file: KJV.sfa
286 bytes table
3190129 bytes output
41.3% compression
```

Decompression Tree

We saw the compression tree for this case on page 6. The decompression tree is a little more complicated. We know the input (number of bits and value) going into the compression phase. As we decompress, one bit is added at each step. We don't know in advance how many bits must be gathered in order to uniquely define the result. We must step through the decompression tree one level at a time, as we roll in each additional bit. We exit the loop when the end of a branch is reached.

Arrays aren't trees. Memory is stored in blocks and traversed by sequential indices. We don't want to devote a huge block of memory large enough to contain every possible non-existent branch. We also don't want to have arrays of arrays of arrays and so on for the maximum possible depth of the tree. Instead, we construct a different kind tree—more like a linked list. Every location in the list contains either the index of the next location or a termination flag (-1) to indicate the end of a branch. Indices and lists must be words, as these can exceed 255. The leaf at the end of the branch (our target character) is a byte type.

We will need a structure something like the following:

0	9	?	11	14	?	22	-1	B
1	2	?	12	13	?	23	-1	R
2	5	?	13	-1	H	24	30	?
3	4	?	14	-1	L	25	26	?
4	-1	S	15	24	?	26	29	?
5	8	?	16	17	?	27	28	?
6	7	?	17	20	?	28	-1	T
7	-1	E	18	19	?	29	-1	Y
8	-1	b	19	-1	A	30	-1	O
9	15	?	20	23	?			
10	11	?	21	22	?			

Each block in the table above consists of three elements. The first is for information only and is not stored in memory. The second is either the index of the next location or −1. The target characters are found only next to the −1s. The table is wrapped into three parts to save space on the page and does not reflect how the table is stored in memory. This is how the list works...

From the preceding table S is 11. The first two entries in the table above are 9 and 2. If zero jump to 9. If one jump to 2. We have 1, so we are now at index 2, which is 5 and 4. If zero jump to 5. If one jump to 4. We have a second 1, so we are now at index 4. Index 4 is −1, so we are at the end of the tree and the leaf is S.

E is 101. The first two entries in the table are 9 and 2. We have 1, so we jump to index 2. At index 2, we have 5 and 4. We have 0, so we jump to 4. At index 4, we have −1, so we are at the end of the branch and the leaf is E.

The decompression tree (named eert) is straightforward:

```
#define lb 12
struct{byte b,c;dword i,j;}eert[(2<<lb)-2];
void DecompressionTree()
  {
  dword i,j,k,l,m,n;
  for(i=j=0,k=m=2;i<lb;i++,k+=k)
    {
    for(l=0;l<k;l++,j++)
      {
      eert[j].i=m++;
      eert[j].j=m++;
      }
    }
  for(i=0;i<trees;i++)
    {
    for(m=1,j=k=0;j<tree[i].b;j++,m<<=1)
```

```
   {
   l=k;
   if(tree[i].l&m)
       {
       n=1;
       k=eert[k].j;
       }
   else
       {
       n=0;
       k=eert[k].i;
       }
   }
  if(n)
   {
   eert[l].j=-1;
   eert[l].c=tree[i].c;
   }
  else
   {
   eert[l].i=-1;
   eert[l].b=tree[i].c;
   }
  }
 }
```

The expansion walks back up the decompression tree

```
void Expand()
 {
 byte b;
 dword i,m;
 for(m=1,i=0;m;m<<=1)
   {
   if(buf.m==0)
     {
     buf.m=1;
     if(++buf.p>=sizeof(buf.i))
       {
       buf.p=0;
       fread(buf.i,1,sizeof(buf.i),fi);
       }
     }
   if(buf.i[buf.p]&buf.m)
     {
     b=eert[i].c;
     i=eert[i].j;
     }
   else
     {
     b=eert[i].b;
```

11

```
      i=eert[i].i;
      }
   buf.m<<=1;
   if(i==-1)
      goto end;
   }
   printf("code not found!\n");
   exit(0);
end:
   buf.o[buf.q]=b;
   if(++buf.q>=sizeof(buf.o))
      {
      fwrite(buf.o,1,sizeof(buf.o),fo);
      buf.q=0;
      }
   }
```

Chapter 4. Huffman Trees

Huffman trees are similar to Shannon-Fano trees, except that they are built from the bottom up, instead of from the top down. As a result, they just happen to be optimal—something Shannon and Fano tried to achieve, but were not successful. Huffman was a student of Fano and the *trees* started as a class assignment. Fano recognized the importance of Huffman's discovery and it was soon published.[6]

As before, we tally the byte count and sort the results. Then, beginning with the two least-frequently-occurring *leaves*, create a *branch*. Create another branch containing two more unlikely leaves. Combine the branches, working upward, bringing in one or two, depending on which yields a smaller sum. The tree for SHE SELLS SEA SHELLS BY THE SEA SHORE is:

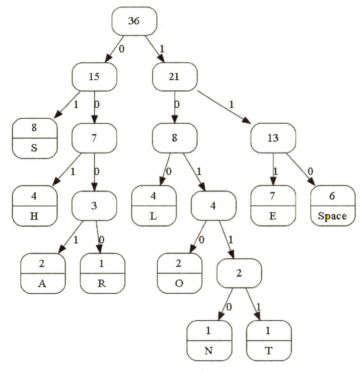

This is the *static* Huffman method, as the tree is built once and doesn't change. We will consider dynamic and adaptive versions of the Huffman algorithm in subsequent chapters. You will find the code (huff.c) and associated

---

[6] Huffman, D. A.,"A Method for the Construction of Minimum-Redundancy Codes," *Proceedings of the IEEE*, Vol. 40, No. 9, pp. 1098-1101, 1952.

files in the folder examples\huff. We can compare the actual effectiveness of this algorithm to the Shannon-Fano by running the same cases:

```
C:\examples\huff>huff c seashells.txt seashells.huf
static Huffman compression utility
input file: seashells.txt
output file: seashells.huf
37 bytes in
228 bytes out
compression -516.2%

C:\examples\huff>huff c GettysburgAddress.txt Gettysbu
rgAddress.huf
static Huffman compression utility
input file: .GettysburgAddress.txt
output file: GettysburgAddress.huf
1578 bytes in
1139 bytes out
compression 27.8%

C:\examples\huff>huff c WitchesBrew.txt WitchesBrew.huf
static Huffman compression utility
input file: WitchesBrew.txt
output file: WitchesBrew.huf
1302 bytes in
1026 bytes out
compression 21.2%

C:\examples\huff>huff c KJV.txt KJV.huf
static Huffman compression utility
input file: KJV.txt
output file: KJV.huf
5436101 bytes in
3186264 bytes out
compression 41.4%
```

Building a static Huffman compression tree is simple:

```
void BuildCompressionTree()
  {
  int i;
  dword j;
  while(buf.d!=1)
    {
    j=huff.h[1];
    huff.h[1]=huff.h[buf.d--];
    ReHeap(1);
    i=buf.d+asize-1;
    huff.n[i]=huff.n[huff.h[1]]+huff.n[j];
    huff.i[j]=i;
    huff.i[huff.h[1]]=-i;
```

```
   huff.h[1]=i;
   ReHeap(1);
   }
 huff.i[asize]=0;
 }
```

Expanding (decompressing) is even simpler with this tree structure:

```
byte ExpandBit()
 {
 buf.m>>=1;
 if(buf.m==0)
   {
   buf.b=fgetc(fi);
   buf.i++;
   buf.m=0x80;
   }
 return(buf.b&buf.m);
 }

void ExpandFile()
 {
 dword i=1;
 dword bout=0;
 while(1)
   {
   i<<=1;
   if(ExpandBit())
     i|=1;
   if(huff.i[i]<=0)
     {
     fputc(-huff.i[i],fo);
     if((++bout)==buf.o)
       return;
     i=1;
     }
   else
     i=huff.i[i];
   }
 }
```

The first two compressed files are actually larger than S-F compression. The last is only slightly smaller. This is an interesting point: just because the tree is optimum doesn't mean that the compressed file will be shorter. This is one of the many examples in life when theory and practice don't exactly coincide.

Chapter 5. Splay Trees

The concept of splay trees is very similar to Shannon-Fano and Huffman encoding in that it has a tree structure and seeks to take advantage of disparity in the frequency of occurrence of the data on a byte-by-byte basis. Splay trees were first developed by Sleator and Tarjan.[7] Splay trees are most often continuously updated during the compression process, making this the first adaptive or dynamic algorithm presented here, although both Shannon-Fano and Huffman can be made dynamic.

We must first initialize the tree. This choice can make a difference when compressing small text files. As bytes of data are added, these are moved to increasingly more probable locations so that the tree structure naturally adjusts to the specific data. It might be possible to fabricate an input file that would arrive at a final splay tree equivalent to a S-F or Huffman tree. Perhaps some graduate student has undertaken this interesting, but pointless, exercise. The process of moving leaves up or down the branches of the splay tree is called by several different names in the literature, but these all describe the same process. We need not update the entire splay tree with each byte, as this would be unnecessary—even counterproductive. We simply update the one branch.

Splay trees are graphically very similar to S-F and Huffman trees, so there's no point drawing one here. The dynamic updating of the tree is easily implemented. You can find the code (splay.c) and associated files in the folder examples\splay.

```
void UpdateTree(byte b)
  {
  dword i,j,k,l;
  k=b+255;
  while(k)
    {
    i=tree.t[k];
    if(i)
      {
      j=tree.t[i];
      l=tree.l[j];
      if(i==l)
        {
        l=tree.r[j];
        tree.r[j]=k;
        }
      else
        tree.l[j]=k;
      if(k==tree.l[i])
        tree.l[i]=l;
```

---

[7] Sleator, D. D. and Tarjan, R. E., "Self-Adjusting Binary Search Trees," *Journal of the ACM*, Vol. 32, No. 3, pp. 652–686, 1985.

```
          else
            tree.r[i]=1;
          tree.t[k]=(byte)j;
          tree.t[l]=(byte)i;
          k=j;
          }
        else
          k=i;
        }
    }

void PutByte(byte b)
  {
  if(buf.q>=sizeof(buf.o))
      {
      fwrite(buf.o,1,buf.q,fo);
      buf.w+=buf.q;
      buf.q=0;
      }
  buf.o[buf.q++]=b;
  }

void CompressByte(byte b)
  {
  dword i,k,j;
  i=b+255;
  j=0;
  while(i)
      {
      k=tree.t[i];
      tree.u[j++]=(tree.r[k]==i);
      i=k;
      }
  tree.m=max(tree.m,j);
  while(j--)
      {
      if(tree.u[j])
        buf.b|=buf.m;
      buf.m<<=1;
      if(buf.m==0)
          {
          PutByte(buf.b);
          buf.m=1;
          buf.b=0;
          }
      }
  UpdateTree(b);
  }
```

Decompressing the data is also straightforward:

```
byte GetByte()
  {
  if(buf.p>=buf.l)
    {
    buf.l=fread(buf.i,1,sizeof(buf.i),fi);
    buf.p=0;
    }
  return(buf.i[buf.p++]);
  }

void OutByte(byte b)
  {
  if(buf.q>=sizeof(buf.c))
    {
    fwrite(buf.o,1,buf.q,fo);
    buf.q=0;
    }
  buf.o[buf.q++]=b;
  }

byte ExpandByte()
  {
  dword i=0;
  while(i<255)
    {
    buf.m<<=1;
    if(buf.m==0)
      {
      buf.c=GetByte();
      buf.m=1;
      }
    if(buf.c&buf.m)
      i=tree.r[i];
    else
      i=tree.l[i];
    }
  i-=255;
  UpdateTree((byte)i);
  return((byte)i);
  }
```

The compression effectiveness for the same three files is shown below:

```
C:\examples\splay>splay c GettysburgAddress.txt
   GettysburgAddress.spl
Splay Tree Compression Utility
input file: GettysburgAddress.txt
output file: GettysburgAddress.spl
1578 bytes in
```

18

```
1070 bytes out
compression 32.2%
20 depth of tree

C:\examples\splay>splay c WitchesBrew.txt
   WitchesBrew.spl
Splay Tree Compression Utility
input file: WitchesBrew.txt
output file: WitchesBrew.spl
1302 bytes in
965 bytes out
compression 25.9%
16 depth of tree

C:\examples\splay>splay c KJV.txt KJV.spl
Splay Tree Compression Utility
input file: KJV.txt
output file: KJV.spl
5436101 bytes in
3816937 bytes out
compression 29.8%
26 depth of tree
```

Chapter 6. Arithmetic Compression

We next discuss what is called *arithmetic* encoding or compression. This technique was first published by Rissanen[8] and further developed by Langdon.[9] One might arrive at this strategy along several paths. It is most often presented in terms of fractions and floating-point numbers in particular, but this can be somewhat confusing, as floating-point number representations are generally associated with limited precision and we are seek a *lossless* compression, implicitly requiring an exact representation.

While presenting arithmetic encoding, it is often mentioned that many of the fractional values are not used, suggesting that we might eliminate them and save space. An examination of the compression tree structure of the three preceding algorithms will reveal that there are often many possible unused leaves and branches on the tree, but this is not the wizardry behind the arithmetic method.

Arithmetic compression uses fractions (i.e., ratio of two integers). The resulting quotient determines the selection. Precise values of the numerator and denominator are not the goal—the quotient is. Several—perhaps many—different combinations of numerator and denominator can result in the same quotient and this is how even more compression is possible. This is illustrated in the following figure:

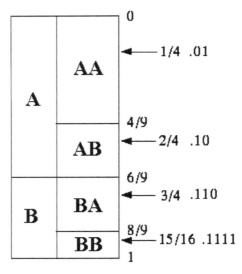

---

[8] Rissanen, J. J., "Generalized Kraft Inequality and Arithmetic Coding," *IBM Journal of Research & Development*, Vol. 20, pp. 198-203, 1976.

[9] Rissanen, J. J. and Langdon, G. G., Jr., "Arithmetic Coding," *IBM Journal of Research & Development*, Vol. 23, pp. 149-162, 1979.

You can find the code (arith.c) and associated files in folder examples\arith. The encoding process is not unlike the previous three:

```c
void Encode(FILE*stream,ARI*a)
  {
  dword range;
  range=(dword)(mask.h-mask.l)+1;
  mask.h=mask.l+(word)((range*a->h)/a->w-1);
  mask.l=mask.l+(word)((range*a->l)/a->w);
  while(1)
    {
    if((mask.h&0x8000)==(mask.l&0x8000))
      {
      bout(stream,mask.h&0x8000);
      while(mask.u>0)
        {
        bout(stream,~mask.h&0x8000);
        mask.u--;
        }
      }
    else if((mask.l&0x4000)&&(!(mask.h&0x4000)))
      {
      mask.u+=1;
      mask.l&=0x3FFF;
      mask.h|=0x4000;
      }
    else
      return;
    mask.l<<=1;
    mask.h<<=1;
    mask.h|=1;
    }
  }
```

The arithmetic codes are accumulated in like manner:

```c
void Accumulate(int a)
  {
  int i;
  for(a++;a<=256;a++)
    bufr.t[a]++;
  if(bufr.t[256]==mbuf)
    {
    for(i=0;i<=256;i++)
      {
      bufr.t[i]/=2;
      if(bufr.t[i]<=bufr.t[i-1])
        bufr.t[i]=bufr.t[i-1]+1;
      }
    }
  }
```

Results for the same three test case text files are as follows:

```
compressing GettysburgAddress.txt to
    GettysburgAddress.xtx
1578 bytes in
997 bytes out
compression 36.8%

compressing WitchesBrew.txt to WitchesBrew.xtx
1302 bytes in
877 bytes out
compression 32.6%

compressing KJV.txt to KJV.xtx
5436101 bytes in
3161385 bytes out
compression 41.8%
```

5-Way Comparison

A comparison of these first four compression methods and WinZip® is given in the following table:

Comparison of Compression Algorithms

Text	uncompressed	S-F	Huff	Splay	Arith	WinZip
input and output file sizes						
Sea Shells	32	54	228	37	37	29
Gettysburg Address	1,578	1,047	1,139	1,070	992	815
Witches Brew	1,302	938	1,026	965	872	650
KJV	5,436,101	3,190,129	3,186,264	3,816,937	3,161,380	1,744,849
CFR	668,655,333	399,337,440	398,468,238	460,742,478	390,686,677	153,169,891
compression achieved						
Sea Shells	32	-68.8%	-612.5%	-15.6%	-15.6%	9.4%
Gettysburg Address	1,578	33.7%	27.8%	32.2%	37.1%	48.4%
Witches Brew	1,302	28.0%	21.2%	25.9%	33.0%	50.1%
KJV	5,436,101	41.3%	41.4%	29.8%	41.8%	67.9%
CFR	668,655,333	40.3%	40.4%	31.1%	41.6%	77.1%

While this is by no means an exhaustive comparison, we do see that an algorithm that is theoretically superior is not necessarily superior in practice. The arithmetic algorithm achieves the most compression for each of these test cases, which is generally true and why it is so often used.

You will find the US Code of Federal Regulations (CFR) listed just below the KJV. I can't resist using this holy book of bureaucratic incompetence, which contains 38,779 unique misspelled words with a total occurrence of 134,703 times. Some occur quite often. The word "alj" (whatever that means) occurs 8753 times. What a breathtaking example of our tax dollar$ at work!

Chapter 7. Run-Length Encoding

RLE is the simplest way of accounting for repetitive values. It's not particularly useful because most meaningful text or code is not repetitive. Some pictures have areas of repeated colors and it is for this reason that the BMP file format allows for run-length encoding.[10] We will consider it here because it provides a segue into the next group of algorithms.

The Microsoft® BMP RLE convention is a byte (0-255) followed by data. If the first byte is zero, the next group is special, consisting of another byte, indicating the length of the group, followed by literal bytes. The following series of bytes would be ABACI (refer to the ASCII chart on page iv).

00 04 41 42 41 43 49

The following would be AAAABBCCC:

04 41 02 42 03 43

In the standard include file wingdi.h, you will find the following definitions:

```
/* constants for the biCompression field */
#define BI_RGB         0L
#define BI_RLE8        1L
#define BI_RLE4        2L
#define BI_BITFIELDS   3L
#define BI_JPEG        4L
#define BI_PNG         5L
```

These definitions appear just after the core structures:

BITMAPFILEHEADER
BITMAPINFOHEADER

While I wouldn't recommend using any of these besides BI_RGB within a Windows® program unless you've already decoded the image using your own code, it does show that both 4-bit and 8-bit RLE exists. The two work exactly the same except for using nibbles (half-bytes) instead of whole bytes. The algorithm is so simple that I won't bother to list it. You can find the code (rle.c) in the folder examples\rle. The performance is so bad for the previous text examples that we won't list that either. In every case, the "compressed" file is bigger than the original.

RLE does sort of work for some black-and-white images, but not really. I have provided two examples: the Statue of Liberty in gray-scale and the United Nations logo in true black-and white. The results are as follows:

```
C:\examples\RLE>rle c Statue_of_Liberty.bmp
    Statue_of_Liberty.rle
```

---

[10] Don't use RLE with any BMP files in Windows®. While the format is supposed to handle this, in most cases it hasn't been implemented within the applications and will more than likely crash any program you try to use it with other than Paint Shop® or Paintbrush® that went out with NT.

```
Run-Length Encoding File Compression Utility
input file: Statue_of_Liberty.bmp
output file: Statue_of_Liberty.rle
2673078 bytes in
4503589 bytes out
compression -68.5%


C:\examples\RLE>rle c United_Nations.bmp
    United_Nations.rle
Run-Length Encoding File Compression Utility
input file: United_Nations.bmp
output file: United_Nations.rle
1257678 bytes in
54777 bytes out
compression 95.6%
```

The 256 shades of gray JPEG of the Statue of Liberty is only 364,100 bytes compared to the RLE, which is 4,503,589 bytes. The 2-color GIF of the UN seal is only 31,392 bytes compared to 54,777 for the RLE. You can see from these examples why this algorithm is not used for general purposes or even pictures. Still, it introduces the subject of repeated bytes, which is the simplest type of pattern.

Raster Metafiles

Another graphics file format that uses run-length encoding is the Raster Metafile. The RM format was developed at the NASA Langley Research Center in the early 1989 to store animations.[11] RM files predated the prevalence of GIFs on the Internet, else there would have been insufficient motivation for NASA's efforts. Earlier versions of Tecplot® (an excellent tool, by the way) output animations as RM files. A viewing tool (Framer®) was provided with Tecplot®. While it no longer comes with the software, it can still be downloaded at:

http://download.tecplot.com/kb/viewing-raster-metafiles-with-framer/framer.exe

Several utilities are described in Appendix B (all provided in the online archive) that transfer images from one format to another, including: BMP, GIF, JPG, and RM.

---

[11] Taylor, N., Everton, E., Randall, D., Gates, R., and Skeens, K., "Raster Metafile and Raster Metafile Translator," NASA TM 102588, September, 1989.
https://ntrs.nasa.gov/archive/nasa/casi.ntrs.nasa.gov/19900008850.pdf

Chapter 8. Dictionary Compression

We will next consider simple dictionary compression. In so doing, we assume everything is a word, including numbers. The process is simple: read through the file, making a list of unique words then replace the words with their location in the dictionary. We then create an output file with the list of words followed by the indices. If there were no more than 65,535 words, we could use 16-bit integers; otherwise, we would need 32-bit. Because the words (and indices) occur at different frequency, we could pass the indices through an additional compression step, using one of the previously discussed methods. This is the most common way of creating a general-purpose compression utility.

We will start with the first step: the dictionary or list of words. You can find all of the files in folder examples\dict. The first program (unique.c) finds, sorts, and lists the unique words in a text file. The unique words in the Gettysburg Address are:

But Four God It Now The We a above add advanced ago all
altogether and any are as battlefield be before birth brave brought
but by can cannot cause civil come conceived consecrate
consecrated continent created dead dedicate dedicated detract
devotion did died do earth endure engaged equal far fathers field
final fitting for forget forth fought freedom from full gave
government great ground hallow have here highly honored in
increased is it larger last liberty little live lives living long measure
men met might nation never new nobly nor not note of on or our
people perish place poor portion power proper proposition rather
remaining remember resolve resting say score sense seven shall
should so struggled take task testing that the their these they this
those thus to under unfinished upon us vain war we what whether
which who will work world years

The most common are (with occurrence):

that	12
we	8
to	8
the	8
here	8
a	7
this	6
and	6
for	5
nation	5
of	5
have	5

The unique words in the witches brew are:

'tis Add Adder's Boil Cool Days Ditch Double Eye Fillet Finger Fire For Gall Harpier In Jew Like Liver Lizard's Make Nose Of Root Round Scale Scene Sliver'd Swelter'd Tartar's Then Thrice Toad Turk Wool a about and babe baboon's bake bat birth blaspheming blind blood boil brinded broth bubble burn by caldron cat charm charmed cauldron cold cries dark deliver'd digg'd dog double drab dragon eclipse entrails fenny firm first fork frog go goat good got gruel gulf has hath hedge hell hemlock in ingredients is it laid leg lips maw mew'd moon's mummy newt nights of once one our owlet's pig poison'd pot powerful ravin'd salt sea shark slab sleeping slips snake sting stone strangled that the thereto thick thirty thou throw tiger's time toe toil tongue tooth trouble under venom whin'd wing with wolf worm's yew

There are 17,195 unique words in the KJV, the most often occurring are:

the	72,405
and	46,821
of	40,510
to	16,594
that	15,721
in	14,699
And	14,057
he	11,561
shall	10,870
unto	10,074
his	10,053
I	9807
a	9806
for	8796

There are quite a few (6267) hapaxes (words that occur only once). Simply using a dictionary like this even for text file compression without something on the back end to compress the integers is not at all effective, as indicated by the following examples:

```
static dictionary compression utility
input file: GettysburgAddress.txt
output file: GettysburgAddress.dic
1578 bytes in
2058 bytes out
compression -30.4%

static dictionary compression utility
input file: WitchesBrew.txt
output file: WitchesBrew.dic
```

```
1302 bytes in
1734 bytes out
compression -33.2%

static dictionary compression utility
input file: KJV.txt
output file: KJV.dic
5436101 bytes in
4214656 bytes out
compression 22.5%
```

These results are using short (16-bit) integers. The output files would be twice as large with 32-bit integers. We are also limited in the number of unique words when using 16-bit integers. While this may not be effective by itself, consider compressing the result again with the arithmetic algorithm from before:

```
arithmetic compression utility
input file: kjv.dic
output file: kjv.ari
compressing
4214656 bytes in
2564731 bytes out
compression 39.1%
(total compression 58.2%)
```

The dictionary compression followed by an arithmetic compression result (2,564,731 bytes) is significantly better at 58.2% than the Shannon-Fano, Huffman, arithmetic, or splay result alone. WinZip® does better (67.9%), for the reasons we will see in the next chapters.

Chapter 9. Ring Compression

Rather than starting with a static dictionary and assuming a file contains text, it is more general to presume a file contains strings—text or binary doesn't matter. For example, the word "another" contains a, an, not, other, the, and her. We need not keep everything in the dictionary, only enough to obtain an optimal result, which we might determine by testing the algorithm on many files. We might also find it advantageous to update the dictionary as we read the file. The simplest way to do this would be add new information as it is gathered and push older (or the oldest) information out. Rather than moving the data each time, it makes more sense to wrap the dictionary around in a circle and just keep track of the current location. The result is a *ring*.

The secret to this method of compression is finding the longest matching string already in the ring. This yields a position and length. Put that information in the output file. If there is no match, move the target string into the ring and store it's position and location. Decompression is the reverse: read the position and length, transfer the matching string, and update the ring. There are several strategies for initializing the ring, replacing parts of the ring, how big to make the ring, etc. This method was first proposed by Ziv and Lempel in 1977.[12] The method (called LZ77) was refined and published a year later.[13] The method was later modified by Storer and Szymanski (LZSS) and published in 1982.[14] It was again modified by Welch (LZW) and published in 1984.[15] We will consider the last two of these, as the nuances are not that important.

LZSS

It makes sense to have a ring length that is a power of 2, as the index can be expressed without wasting bits. This length is typically 4096 (12 bits) or 8192 (13 bits). The match length is also typically a power of 2, perhaps 8 (3 bits) or 16 (4 bits). It may also be advantageous conserve space and improve speed of manipulation to select these to such that they add up to a unit native to the hardware, for instance, 12+4=16 bits (a short integer) or 13+3=16 bits.

Lempel and Ziv originally encoded all strings in this way, including single characters. Storer and Szymanski, noting that individual characters coded in this manner would be larger than the original size. Therefore, they added the option of uncoded (literal) characters. In our implementation (lzss.c in folder examples\

---

[12] Ziv, J. and Lempel, A., "A Universal Algorithm for Sequential Data Compression," IEEE Transactions on Information Theory, Vol. 23, No. 4, pp. 337–343, 1977.

[13] Ziv, J. and Lempel, A., "Compression of Individual Sequences via Variable-Rate Coding," IEEE Transactions on Information Theory, Vol. 24, No. 5, p: 530, 1978.

[14] Storer, J. A. and Szymanski, T. G., "Data Compression via Textual Substitution," Journal of the ACM, Vol. 29, No. 4, pp. 928–951, 1982.

[15] Welch, T., "A Technique for High-Performance Data Compression," Computer, Vol. 17, No. 6, pp. 8–19, 1984.

lzss), we will use a ring of length 4096 and a match length of up to 16. We will also read the file in two blocks of 8096 bytes so that we can search for matches. Once we get past the first block, we shift it over and read in another block.

By far, the most computationally-intensive part of this process is searching for matches. We must organize the data (ring and input buffers) so as to take advantage of the fast library routines. These take special advantage of the Intel® hardware instruction set; otherwise, we would resort to inline assembler. Finding the first matching character takes a lot longer than extending the match, so we begin with memchr and continue with optimized code, locating and saving the longest match:

```
void MemFind()
  {
  byte bite;
  word i,nmat;
  register byte*iptr,*rptr;
  register word l,lmax;
  ring.m=ring.y=0;
  if(ring.l<2)
    return;
  if(ring.x-ring.q<2)
    return;
  lmax=ring.x-ring.q;
  lmax=min(lmax,16);
  lmax=min(lmax,ring.l);
  nmat=ring.l-lmax+1;
  bite=bufr.i[ring.q];
  i=0;
  while(i<nmat)
    {
    rptr=memchr(ring.b+i,bite,ring.l-i);
    if(rptr==NULL)
      return;
    l=1;
    i=rptr-ring.b;
    iptr=bufr.i+ring.q+1;
    rptr++;
    while(*rptr++==*iptr++)
      if(++l>=lmax)
        break;
    if(l>ring.y)
      {
      ring.y=l;
      ring.m=i;
      if(l>=lmax)
        return;
      }
    i++;
```

```
      }
  }

void ForFind()
  {
  register byte*iptr,*rptr;
  register word l,lmax;
  word i,nmat;
  ring.m=ring.y=0;
  if(ring.l<2)
    return;
  if(ring.x-ring.q<2)
    return;
  lmax=ring.x-ring.q;
  lmax=min(lmax,16);
  lmax=min(lmax,ring.l):
  nmat=ring.l-lmax+1;
  for(i=0;i<nmat;i++)
    {
    rptr=ring.b+i;
    iptr=bufr.i+ring.q;
    for(l=0;l<lmax;l++)
      if(*rptr++!=*iptr++)
        break;
    if(l>ring.y)
      {
      ring.y=l;
      ring.m=i;
      if(ring.y>=lmax)
        return;
      }
    }
  }
```

Results for the same three text files are as follows:

```
Lempel-Ziv-Storer-Szymaski file compression
input file: GettysburgAddress.txt
output file: GettysburgAddress.xtx
1578 bytes in
1147 bytes out
compression 27.3%

Lempel-Ziv-Storer-Szymaski file compression
input file: WitchesBrew.txt
output file: WitchesBrew.xtx
1302 bytes in
980 bytes out
compression 24.7%

Lempel-Ziv-Storer-Szymaski file compression
```

```
input file: KJV.txt
output file: KJV.xtx
5436101 bytes in
2331876 bytes out
compression 57.1%
```

We see from these examples (plus the CFR) that LZSS is better on (byte-weighted) average (64.2%) than any of the other methods discussed except WinZip®.

LZW

Welch's modification encodes strings as 12-bit codes. The codes from 0 to 255 represent single-character literal bytes. The codes 256 through 4095 correspond to locations in the ring, which is continuously updated. You will find the code (lzw.c) in folder examples\lzw. The compression sequence is very similar to LZSS:

```
void CompressFile()
  {
  word i,l,lmat,r,rmat;
  dword binp;
  bufr.q=0;
  ring.m=0x80;
  memcpy(bufr.o,tag,3);
  bufr.k=3;
  *(dword*)(bufr.o+3)=bufr.l;
  bufr.k+=sizeof(dword);
  bufr.x=fread(bufr.i,1,isiz+isiz,fi);
  bufr.y=min(bufr.x,isiz);
  binp=bufr.x;
  while(1)
    {
    if(bufr.j>=bufr.y)
      {
      if(bufr.x<=isiz)
        break;
      memcpy(bufr.i,bufr.i+isiz,isiz);
      bufr.x-=isiz;
      if(bufr.x==isiz)
        {
        memset(bufr.i+isiz,0,isiz);
        bufr.x+=fread(bufr.i+isiz,1,isiz,fi);
        binp+=bufr.x-isiz;
        }
      bufr.j-=isiz;
      bufr.y=min(bufr.x,isiz);
      }
    lmat=0;
    for(r=bufr.i[bufr.j];r<rsiz-lmax;r++)
```

```
        {
        if(ring.b[r]!=bufr.i[bufr.j])
          continue;
        l=1;
        i=bufr.j+1;
        while(i<bufr.x)
          {
          if(bufr.i[i]!=ring.b[r+l])
            break;
          if(++l>=lmax)
            break;
          i++;
          }
        if(l>lmat)
          {
          lmat=l;
          rmat=r;
          if(lmat>=lmax)
            break;
          }
        }
    CompressWord(lmat-1,ring.l);
    CompressWord(rmat,ring.r);
    for(l=0;l<lmat;l++)
      {
      ring.b[ring.p]=bufr.i[bufr.j++];
      if(++ring.p>=rsiz)
        ring.p=256;
      }
    }
  while(ring.m!=0x80)
    CompressBit(0);
  if(bufr.k>0)
    {
    fwrite(bufr.o,1,bufr.k,fo);
    bufr.m+=bufr.k;
    }
  }
```

We see from the following same three examples that LZW doesn't quite achieve the compression ratios of LZSS. For the following three plus the KJV and CFR, the weighted average for LZW is 62.7%, while for LZSS is 64.2%.

```
Lempel-Ziv-Welch file compression
input file: ..\examples\text\GettysburgAddress.txt
output file: GettysburgAddress.xtx
1578 bytes in
1223 bytes out
compression 22.5%
```

```
Lempel-Ziv-Welch file compression
input file: ..\examples\text\WitchesBrew.txt
output file: WitchesBrew.xtx
1302 bytes in
1081 bytes out
compression 17.0%

Lempel-Ziv-Welch file compression
input file: KJV.txt
output file: KJV.xtx
5436101 bytes in
2401323 bytes out
compression 55.8%
```

If you use these last two programs (lzss.c and lzw.c), you will find that, even though they have been written tightly, execution is quite slow for very large files. This is not due to sloppy programming but the tedious searching for strings. For this reason, successful implementations (e.g., WinZip®) build one or more hash tables to keep track of character positions within the ring. As this is a matter performance and not part of the compression algorithm, we will not implement this process at this point, although I have implemented it elsewhere in utilities that I routinely use.

Chapter 10. Two-Stage Compression

We introduced the concept of two-stage compression on page 27 by recompressing the output of a dictionary algorithm with the arithmetic algorithm to achieve a significantly greater overall compression factor. This is how most popular utilities (e.g., WinZip®) work. The front end is some sort of ring compression and the back end is either Huffman or arithmetic. As we noted in the last chapter that LZSS seems to work better than LZW (at least in my experience) and arithmetic more often than not works better than Huffman. The logical combination is LZSS+Arith. You can find the code (lzari.c) in the folder examples\lzari.

The algorithm used here is simply the combination of the two previously discussed. Rather than writing the intermediate first compression step to a file, reading it back in, and compressing it again, we just send the output of the first to the second via function calls. The code structure is similar and you are welcome to peruse it. Results for the same three test files are as follows:

```
Lempel-Ziv-Storer-Szymaski/Adaptive Arithmetic
    Compression Utility
input file: GettysburgAddress.txt
output file: GettysburgAddress.xtx
1578 bytes in
compressing file
892 bytes out
compression 43.5%

input file: WitchesBrew.txt
output file: WitchesBrew.xtx
1302 bytes in
compressing file
717 bytes out
compression 44.9%

input file: KJV.txt
output file: KJV.xtx
5436101 bytes in
compressing file
2109697 bytes out
compression 61.2%
```

The weighted average compression for these three files plus the CFR is 69.0%, which does exceed the LZSS and LZW alone. If you run the utility, you will notice that it's a lot faster than any of the preceding ones. This is because I have spent a lot more time refining the code than on the others. The previous ones are interesting for the sake of demonstration, but not practical or utilitarian. LZARI, however, has considerable practical use.

The principle compression functions are listed below:

```
void PutByte(byte b)
  {
  lzar.o[lzar.a++]=b;
  }

void PutBit(short bit)
  {
  if(bit)
    lzar.b|=lzar.m;
  if((lzar.m>>=1)==0)
    {
    PutByte(lzar.b);
    lzar.b=0;
    lzar.m=0x80;
    }
  }

void PutBitNotBit(short bit)
  {
  PutBit(bit);
  for(;lzar.f>0;lzar.f--)
    PutBit(!bit);
  }

void UpdateTable(short sym)
  {
  short i,c,ch_i,ch_sym;
  if(lzar.v[0]>=Qmin)
    {
    c=0;
    for(i=Rbeg;i>0;i--)
      {
      lzar.v[i]=c;
      c+=(lzar.w[i]=(lzar.w[i]+1)>>1);
      }
    lzar.v[0]=c;
    }
  for(i=sym;lzar.w[i]==lzar.w[i-1];i--)
    continue;
  if(i<sym)
    {
    ch_i=lzar.y[i];
    ch_sym=lzar.y[sym];
    lzar.y[i]=ch_sym;
    lzar.y[sym]=ch_i;
    lzar.c[ch_i]=sym;
    lzar.c[ch_sym]=i;
    }
```

35

```
  lzar.w[i]++;
  while(--i>=0)
    lzar.v[i]++;
  }

void CompressByte(short ch)
  {
  short sym;
  dword Qran;
  sym=lzar.c[ch];
  Qran=lzar.h-lzar.g;
  lzar.h=lzar.g+(Qran*lzar.v[sym-1])/lzar.v[0];
  lzar.g+=(Qran*lzar.v[sym])/lzar.v[0];
  while(1)
    {
    if(lzar.h<=Qmx2)
      PutBitNotBit(0);
    else if(lzar.g>=Qmx2)
      {
      PutBitNotBit(1);
      lzar.g-=Qmx2;
      lzar.h-=Qmx2;
      }
    else if(lzar.g>=Qmx1&&lzar.h<=Qmx3)
      {
      lzar.f++;
      lzar.g-=Qmx1;
      lzar.h-=Qmx1;
      }
    else
      break;
    lzar.g+=lzar.g;
    lzar.h+=lzar.h;
    }
  UpdateTable(sym);
  }

void CompressWord(short position)
  {
  dword Qran;
  Qran=lzar.h-lzar.g;
  lzar.h=lzar.g+(Qran*lzar.u[position])/lzar.u[0];
  lzar.g+=(Qran*lzar.u[position+1])/lzar.u[0];
  while(1)
    {
    if(lzar.h<=Qmx2)
      PutBitNotBit(0);
    else if(lzar.g>=Qmx2)
      {
```

```
            PutBitNotBit(1);
            lzar.g-=Qmx2;
            lzar.h-=Qmx2;
            }
         else if(lzar.g>=Qmx1&&lzar.h<=Qmx3)
            {
            lzar.f++;
            lzar.g-=Qmx1;
            lzar.h-=Qmx1;
            }
         else
            break;
         lzar.g+=lzar.g;
         lzar.h+=lzar.h;
         }
   }
```

The ring and tree functions are:

```
void InitializeTree()
   {
   short i;
   for(i=Rsiz+1;i<=Rsiz+256;i++)
      lzar.t[i]=Rsiz;
   for(i=0;i<Rsiz;i++)
      lzar.d[i]=Rsiz;
   }

void InitializeRing()
   {
   short ch,sym,i;
   lzar.v[Rbeg]=0;
   for(sym=Rbeg;sym>=1;sym--)
      {
      ch=sym-1;
      lzar.c[ch]=sym;
      lzar.y[sym]=ch;
      lzar.w[sym]=1;
      lzar.v[sym-1]=lzar.v[sym]+lzar.w[sym];
      }
   lzar.w[0]=lzar.u[Rsiz]=0;
   for(i=Rsiz;i>=1;i--)
      lzar.u[i-1]=lzar.u[i]+10000/(i+200);
   }

void InsertNode(short r)
   {
   short i,p,cmp=1,temp;
   byte*key;
   key=lzar.r+r;
   p=Rsiz+1+key[0];
```

```
lzar.t[r]=lzar.s[r]=Rsiz;
lzar.l=0;
while(1)
  {
  if(cmp>=0)
    {
    if(lzar.t[p]!=Rsiz)
      p=lzar.t[p];
    else
      {
      lzar.t[p]=r;
      lzar.d[r]=p;
      return;
      }
    }
  else
    {
    if(lzar.s[p]!=Rsiz)
      p=lzar.s[p];
    else
      {
      lzar.s[p]=r;
      lzar.d[r]=p;
      return;
      }
    }
  for(i=1;i<Rmax;i++)
    if((cmp=key[i]-lzar.r[p+i])!=0)
      break;
  if(i>Rmin)
    {
    if(i>lzar.l)
      {
      lzar.z=(r-p)&(Rsiz-1);
      if((lzar.l=i)>=Rmax)
        break;
      }
    else if(i==lzar.l)
      {
      if((temp=(r-p)&(Rsiz-1))<lzar.z)
        lzar.z=temp;
      }
    }
  }
lzar.d[r]=lzar.d[p];
lzar.s[r]=lzar.s[p];
lzar.t[r]=lzar.t[p];
lzar.d[lzar.s[p]]=r;
lzar.d[lzar.t[p]]=r;
```

```c
  if(lzar.t[lzar.d[p]]==p)
    lzar.t[lzar.d[p]]=r;
  else
    lzar.s[lzar.d[p]]=r;
  lzar.d[p]=Rsiz;
  }

void DeleteNode(short p)
  {
  short q;
  if(lzar.d[p]==Rsiz)
    return;
  if(lzar.t[p]==Rsiz)
    q=lzar.s[p];
  else if(lzar.s[p]==Rsiz)
    q=lzar.t[p];
  else
    {
    q=lzar.s[p];
    if(lzar.t[q]!=Rsiz)
      {
      do
        {
        q=lzar.t[q];
        }while(lzar.t[q]!=Rsiz);
      lzar.t[lzar.d[q]]=lzar.s[q];
      lzar.d[lzar.s[q]]=lzar.d[q];
      lzar.s[q]=lzar.s[p];
      lzar.d[lzar.s[p]]=q;
      }
    lzar.t[q]=lzar.t[p];
    lzar.d[lzar.t[p]]=q;
    }
  lzar.d[q]=lzar.d[p];
  if(lzar.t[lzar.d[p]]==p)
    lzar.t[lzar.d[p]]=q;
  else
    lzar.s[lzar.d[p]]=q;
  lzar.d[p]=Rsiz;
  }

BLOC LZcompress(BLOC inp)
  {
  short i,len,last;
  byte b;
  static BLOC out;
  union{byte b[4];dword d;}u;
  memset(&out,0,sizeof(BLOC));
  lzar.i=inp.b;
```

```
lzar.j=inp.l;
lzar.e=0;
if((lzar.o=malloc(lzar.j+1024))==NULL)
  return(out);
lzar.f=0;
lzar.a=lzar.b=lzar.g=0;
lzar.m=0x80;
lzar.h=Qmx4;
PutByte(tag[0]);
PutByte(tag[1]);
PutByte(tag[2]);
PutByte(tag[3]);
InitializeRing();
InitializeTree();
lzar.x=0;
lzar.p=Rsiz-Rmax;
memset(lzar.r,' ',lzar.p);
for(len=0;len<Rmax&&lzar.e<lzar.j;len++)
  lzar.r[lzar.p+len]=GetByte();
for(i=1;i<=Rmax;i++)
  InsertNode(lzar.p-i);
InsertNode(lzar.p);
do
  {
  if(lzar.l>len)
    lzar.l=len;
  if(lzar.l<=Rmin)
    {
    lzar.l=1;
    CompressByte(lzar.r[lzar.p]);
    }
  else
    {
    CompressByte(255-Rmin+lzar.l);
    CompressWord(lzar.z-1);
    }
  last=lzar.l;
  for(i=0;i<last&&lzar.e<lzar.j;i++)
    {
    DeleteNode(lzar.x);
    b=GetByte();
    lzar.r[lzar.x]=b;
    if(lzar.x<Rmax-1)
      lzar.r[lzar.x+Rsiz]=b;
    lzar.x=(lzar.x+1)&(Rsiz-1);
    lzar.p=(lzar.p+1)&(Rsiz-1);
    InsertNode(lzar.p);
    }
  while(i++<last)
```

```c
      {
      DeleteNode(lzar.x);
      lzar.x=(lzar.x+1)&(Rsiz-1);
      lzar.p=(lzar.p+1)&(Rsiz-1);
      if(--len)
         InsertNode(lzar.p);
      }
   }while(len>0);
lzar.f++;
if(lzar.g<Qmx1)
   PutBitNotBit(0);
else
   PutBitNotBit(1);
while(lzar.m&0x7F)
   PutBit(0);
u.d=lzar.j;
PutByte(u.b[0]);
PutByte(u.b[1]);
PutByte(u.b[2]);
PutByte(u.b[3]);
out.b=lzar.o;
out.l=lzar.a;
return(out);
}
```

Chapter 11. Zip & Tar

The Zip compression utility was developed by Phil Katz and has been around since 1989. Then it was a DOS® tool and came in two parts as PKZIP and PKUNZIP. I still have copies and they still work on 32-bit versions of Windows®. Due to the large memory access coding, these will not run on any 64-bit version of Windows®. WinZip® was developed by Corel® and first released in 1991. It will run on virtually every version of Windows®. WinZip® will still handle files compressed with PKZIP and the first two letters of every ZIP file are PK.[16]

The ZIP file format is so widely used around the world of computing that it has become the de facto standard, at least for Windows® machines. We will discuss tar and gzip in the next chapter. In the early days of file compression, space was a big issue—both for storage and transmittal. That is less of a concern with each passing year. Keeping groups of files—and even folders—all inside a single archive has become the primary motivation for Zipping. WinZip® does an excellent job of this. For more information, I direct you to their web site:

https://www.winzip.com/

While I have used several other such utilities, including WinRAR® and 7ZIP®, I have seen no compelling reason to prefer these over WinZip®. These are said to have improved security features. I have been working on computers since 1972 and have never gotten a virus because I don't do stupid things like visiting web sites in Belarus, nor do I share my bank account information with the Prime Minister of Nigeria. I also don't double click on smiley faces to get 10% off on my next purchase of any latte over $20. This simply isn't sufficient motivation for me to switch.

miniz

Rich Geldreich has graciously set up a GitHub project for a simple archive utility called miniz that is compatible with the WinZip® file format. You can view the project and download the code at this address:

https://github.com/richgel999/miniz

I give Rich all the credit for developing and supporting this very useful (and CHEAP!) utility. The web site says that miniz has been tested with gcc (the GNU®/LINUX® compiler) and also Visual Studio® (i.e., Microsoft® C). It has been my experience that, if some code was developed by anyone using gcc, you'll be lucky to ever compile it with anything else. I confess to having a strong

---

[16] Note that the first two letters of every DOCX and XLSX file are also PK. If you change the extension to ZIP, you can unzip these and see the raw contents, which is XML—perhaps the stupidest, most bloated, and convoluted format ever devised. Note that Windows® versions beyond XP-SP3 can recognize, create, and open ZIP files.

bias in this area. Any software that I write and/or use must compile with Zortech/Symantec/Digital Mars *and* Microsoft C (after 2005) with the maximum warnings enabled and warnings treated as errors. If it doesn't, you can't be sure of the outcome because of ambiguities in the language, compilers, and hardware. I won't go any further with this tasteless rant. Suffice it to say that miniz required a lot of work to get from where it was to meet this expectation.

mzip

In addition to maintaining and transmitting zipped archives, which can readily be accomplished using WinZip®, I have two other needs: 1) a command line interface that works inside a batch file to facilitate tedious and repetitious tasks and 2) reading and/or writing a file without explicitly unzipping it from inside some other code. I have written a little shell for miniz (just like sfan, huff, arith, splay, lzss, and lzw, already described) to accomplish the first task. I have partitioned off the core routines in miniz to create a static library and accomplish the second task. I'm very reluctant to use DLLs and much prefer static libraries.

You will find all of the mzip code code, library, and include file in folder examples\mzip. In this folder there are also 4 batch files: one to compile the utility, a second to test the utility, a third to compile the library (32-bit and 64-bit versions), and a fourth to compile the test program (ziptest.c) that reads a zip file from an enormous single data statement (the entire KJV, one byte at a time). The test output is:

```
mzip version 2.01
text.zip
sizeby    zipped ratio  mm/dd/yyyy hh:mm:ss filename
    256       261 ( 0%)  06/14/2019 09:50:18 chr256.txt
   1578       815 (43%)  10/22/2014 14:28:12 GettysburgAddress.txt
5436101   1746254 (68%)  06/14/2019 08:35:22 KJV.txt
     37        29 (22%)  06/13/2019 15:05:44 seashells.txt
   1302       650 (50%)  10/22/2014 14:20:06 WitchesBrew.txt
archive contains 5 files
```

Command line options include: -a (add), -d (delete), -l (list), -r (replace), -u (update), and −x (extract). Wild cards (?*) can be used for any of the file names except the archive itself. Unlike the preceding utilities described in this book, mzip handles multiple files and restores file dates, as expected for such a utility.

Tar/Untar/Gzip

To be complete, we must also discuss tar, untar, and gzip. UNIX and LINUX both recognize archives called tar balls. These may or may not be compressed (gzipped). If you are running Windows®, you may have to deal with tar balls and so a utility is required to gather and split these. You will find two codes (tar.c and untar.c) in the folder examples\tar. In the examples\gzip folder, you will find another code (gzip.c), which will compress and decompress these LINUX archives. The original gzip code was developed by Jean-loup

43

Gailly and has been modified to compile with Microsoft® C. You will also find a static library in this folder that can be used to gzip and gunzip files from within some other program. I process many meteorological data files from the National Climate Data Center (a UNIX server), which are gzipped tar balls.[17] The archives contain many thousands of individual files, which I don't care to unzip before reading, so this library enables me to read them without manually untarring them and handling tens of thousands of individual files. The file formats are not particularly interesting, so we won't dwell on them here.

---

[17] You may be interested in this data, which consists of about 30,000 weather stations around the globe. ftp://ftp.ncdc.noaa.gov/pub/data/gsod/

Chapter 12. GIF

The Graphics Interchange Format (GIF) was developed at CompuServe® through a team effort led by Steve Wilhite. The standard was first released in 1987 (called GIF87). The Web was young and transfer rates were slow, while image content was the rage. This provided motivation for image compression. Processors were also slow, which provided motivation for fast and efficient compression. The algorithm chosen for this task is that of LZW, which we covered in Chapter 9. The LZW algorithm is lossless, which makes a big difference compared to lossy compression when it comes to line drawings, charts, and text. Transparency and text labels, along with several other minor enhancements were added two years later, forming GIF89a.

The GIF format supports palette-based images, that is, a fixed-length palette (no larger than 256 entries) consisting of red-green-blue (RGB) values, plus an array of indices into that palette forming the image. This is distinct from 24-bit images in which each pixel potentially has a separate RGB value. Besides compression, perhaps the biggest advantage of the GIF standard was animation. Optimizing, reducing, and/or combining palettes along with transparency can greatly reduce the size compared to the original frames in a static animation.

Animations often have a background that is fairly consistent with most changes occurring in the foreground. The pixels that don't change from one frame to the next are set to transparent. Although the color indices might not be the same along a horizontal line, these might be the same as in the previous frame. Thus, the transparent index may occur far more than any other, plus it may be repeated for a considerable length. This results in excellent compression ratios when using LZW, which is a ring-based algorithm.

The GIF specification also allows for *interlacing*. This option splits the image into eight-pixel-high horizontal strips and packs these separately. This allows you to display the image at increasing levels of detail as it is being received, rather than waiting until the entire file has been transmitted. Interlaced images provided a more immediate presentation when internet speeds seemed glacial compared to current transfer rates. The practice ended long ago, for even the slowest service now is lightning fast compared to the best available in 1987.

While discussing GIF it is worth noting that this very effective and enduring file format sparked one of the most controversial patent battles in the history of the Internet. Welch, in company with what would become Unisys®, filed for a US patent in 1983 and subsequently in several other countries, including: the UK, France, Germany, Italy, Japan, and Canada. CompuServe®, unaware of this restriction, promoted the format online, while Unisys®, the patent holder, demanded royalties for anyone creating or hosting GIF images.

While international mega-corporations appear to dominate much of the Internet in 2019, this was not the case in 1993, when the controversy was at peak. Countless individuals and shoestring upstarts rebelled against fees for any

Web content. The backlash was unexpected and the patents finally expired in 2003 through 2004. While never personally involved with the conflict, this author was quite active on the Web at the time and much influenced by the spirit of free information exchange, eschewing mercenary motives as shameful.

Lossless compression plus animation makes GIF my personal preference for content, as illustrated below. You will find many such images on my web site listed in the Forward. Several utilities are described in Appendix B and included in the online archive that accompanies this text.

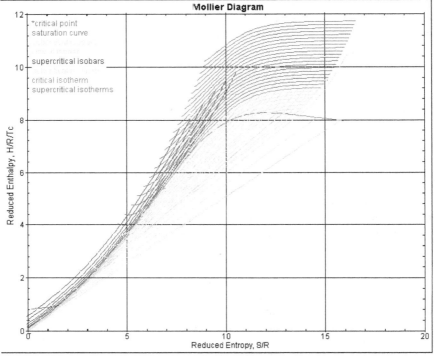

I use a modified version of the gifsicle core code:

http://www.lcdf.org/gifsicle/

which was developed by Eddie Kohler and is available on GetHub at:

https://github.com/kohler/gifsicle

The unmodified code is only marginally compatible with the Microsoft® C compiler and only for 32-bit and not 64-bit compilation. The modified version described in Appendix B works with either. You are welcome to use the modified code but please give Eddie due credit for all his hard work on the front end.

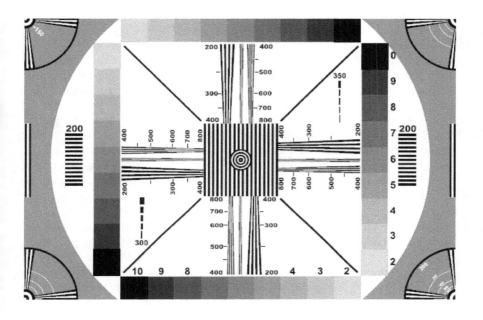

Chapter 13. JPEG

JPEG is the most commonly used method of compression for digital photographs. JPEG is a lossy compression algorithm developed by the Joint Photographic Experts Group. JPEG should not be used for line drawings or anything containing fine detail, such as the graph on the preceding page. JPEG uses a lossy form of compression based on the discrete cosine transform (DCT). This concept treats 8x8 pixel blocks within an image in a pseudo-frequency domain, rather than the two-dimensional spatial domain. This is not a true frequency domain, as the wavelengths associated wit each color in the image is not used in any way. This model is loosely based on human optical perception by placing more importance on trends and hues than sharp edges and intensities.

Much effort went into developing this very complex compression method, which is readily apparent in the various code implementations. The blocks are first transformed into *chroma* components: blue, red, and intensity. These are given the symbols C_B, C_R, and Y, respectively. For a 256-shade gray-scale image, only the Y component is encoded. For full-color images, the C_B and C_R components are encoded separately. C_B and C_R only loosely correspond to blue and red in RGB 24-bit convention. The third component, which would be C_G, is not needed in this representation as $C_G = Y - C_B - C_R$. Various formulae can be found on the Web for converting RGB to CYY. Many of these involve floating-point calculations, which take much longer than integer calculations and also require rounding. The following simple integer calculations are recommended:

$$Y = \frac{54R + 183G + 19B}{256}$$
$$C_B = 128 + \frac{-38R - 74G + 112B}{256}$$
$$C_R = 128 + \frac{112R - 94G - 18B}{256}$$

(13.1)

The denominator above should be 256 instead of 255 because this is 2^8 (or 1<<8 in C) and becomes simply a shift right by 8 bits. On Intel® processors, this is taking the high byte and discarding the low byte of a 16-bit unsigned integer, which requires no processing time at all.

Many graphics tools (e.g., Paint Shop Pro®, my personal favorite) provide channel splitting from 24-bit color to RGB (red, green, and blue) or HSL (hue, saturation, and lightness) or CMYK (cyan, magenta, yellow, and black). Few provide splitting into YC_BC_R, which is the first step in preparing a JPG. Clearly, all of these programs perform this step internally. There is simply no clear purpose for doing so interactively, as nobody uses this split for anything else. See Appendix F for code. Consider the following full color (24-bit) image:

The RGB and YC_BC_R split are shown side-by-side on the next page. This particular representation is unusual, as I have used explicit shades of red, green, and blue rather than gray for each of the components except the Y, which has been left gray. This is for illustration purposes and not how the pixel data are stored. The two-dimensional discrete cosine transform (DCT) takes the following form:

$$I_{XY} = \frac{1}{norm} \sum_{x=0}^{x=7} \sum_{y=0}^{y=7} i_{XY} \cos\left[\frac{(2x+1)u\pi}{16}\right] \cos\left[\frac{(2y+1)v\pi}{16}\right] \quad (13.2)$$

where x is the horizontal position (left to right) within the 8x8 cell, Y is the vertical position (top to bottom) within the 8x8 cell, i_{XY} is the intensity of the cell at X,Y, u and v are the spatial frequencies (both vary from 0 to 7). The norm is either $1/\sqrt{2}$ if u (or v) equals 0; otherwise it is 1.

Several more carefully crafted steps yield the striking compression ratios typical of JPEG. The DCT is performed with approximate, rather than full floating-point calculations. The results are then rounded to integers with assumed divisors. These are stored in a zigzag ordered block. The innovative ordering actually makes a difference in the compression achieved. The last step is Huffman encoding, as described in Chapter 4. While this requires an extremely complicated algorithm, it achieves far more compression than could ever be achieved with any lossless compression of the same image as 24-bit RGBs or 8-bit palette indices. The 8x8=64 values from the preceding formula

(Equation 13.2) are rounded to integers and arranged in triangular form, as shown below:

```
-17
-18 -14
 11  -5  11
  1   2  10  27
  7 -17  29 -11  19
 -3  17  22 -30  14   0
 23  -6 -18  15   0   0   0
  1   6  15   0   0   0   0   0
-31 -20   0   0   0   0   0
-17   0   0   0   0   0
  0   0   0   0   0
  0   0   0   0
  0   0   0
  0   0
  0
```

Many of these values round down to zero, which is why the compression is so effective. The order in which the values are stored also makes a difference. This order forms a zigzag pattern:

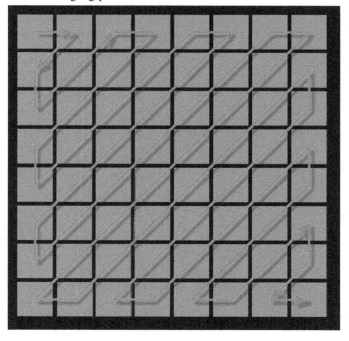

I use a much-modified version of the code developed by Thomas G. Lane, whose original work is available on GetHub:

https://github.com/mackyle/jpeg

My implementation also includes modified elements from Rich Geldreich's small JPEG decoder, also available on GetHub:

https://github.com/richgel999/jpeg-compressor

The original code (which I downloaded back in 1997 and have been using ever since), comes in over one hundred bits and pieces that choke the Microsoft® C compiler. This is a common problem with software on the Web intended for compilation with gcc and use on LINUX—still with only 3.3% market share. The modified version you will find in the archive accompanying this text consists of a single file that meets the criterion: compile with maximum warning level and warnings treated as errors. See Appendix B for more details.

Chapter 14. MP3

The MP3 audio compression and associated file format was developed by Moving Picture Experts Group (MPEG) and initially release in 1993. It was originally designated MPEG-1 (or MPEG–2) Audio Layer III and later shortened. MP3 uses lossy data-compression through approximation as well as discarding parts of the data, which are considered less important or cannot be detected by the human ear. Sound data are subjected to what is called psychoacoustic analysis—an elaborate term referring to the hearing capability and perception of most humans. Typical compression ratios are 75% to 95%, much like that achieved with JPG encoding of photographs.

Sound data on a CD has the form of literal digitized intensities at some specified sampling rate (e.g., 8, 12, 16, 24, 32, or 48 kHz). There may be a single (mono) or two (stereo) data streams. MP3 roughly follows this same categorization, only compressed by transforming the data from the temporal (time) to tonal (frequency) domain. Playback involves the reverse transformation into the time domain While MP3 was only supported by a few software and hardware products in the 1990s, it is now ubiquitous. The Web abounds with free MP3 software, music is readily available, and so are players. Virtually all cellular phones and smart devices recognize the format. A Fast Fourier Transform (FFT) is used to convert the sound data from the time to frequency domain, followed by integer approximation and truncation, as well as filtering. Specific details of the file format and the transformation process will be left to the many web sites devoted to this subject.

Chapter 15. Basic Encryption

What's the easiest way to encrypt data? You might simply use a compression algorithm that nobody else uses. Where might you find such a thing? Shannon-Fano is a good example—just search the Web for "nobody uses this algorithm because it's slower than a herd of snails" or "isn't nearly as effective as the bobo3 algorithm" or "this algorithm is totally impractical and only of historical interest." I could just stop right here, but I won't.

If you are really concerned about some particular data, merely putting a password on it (like in a ZIP file or some similar archive format) is ineffective. A brief search of the Web will quickly lead you to somebody who has cracked all of these programs. Some of the most pathetic security measures are those of Microsoft® documents and spreadsheets. A Google™ search for "remove ms word password" turns up 51.6 million hits. By comparison "remove excel password" is much more secure (NOT!) at only 31.2 million hits. You can easily create a bootable memory stick that will remove the Windows® administrator password and let you into any machine using that operating system.

Windows® built-in file encryption with a certificate is one of the most annoying things I've ever had to deal with from a company known for creating annoying products. One day my machine informed me that my certificate had expired. I needed a new one, as mine couldn't be extended. I was told to get a new certificate from the company that issued me the currently expired one. I issued the certificate to myself! I didn't get it from anyone. Windows® created it for me when I first encrypted the drive. I would have been totally screwed once again, except that I'm OCD when it comes to backups and backups of backups and so on. After trying several "guaranteed" fixes that didn't work, I reformatted the drive and copied everything over again from one of my many backups. Not doing that again!

Ralphie's Little Orphan Annie Decoder Ring

Some people—albeit those with a warped sense of humor—consider this the most famous encryption tool and message sequence of all time, eclipsing even the enigma machine pictured on page ii. In the 1983 film, *A Christmas Story*, Ralphie Parker decodes a top-secret message from Little Orphan Annie using the mail-order decoder ring. This urgent message turns out to be a commercial plug for the radio show's sponsor, Ovaltine®, a malt drink mix sold by Nestlé®. The message is, "Be Sure To Drink Your Ovaltine." If you haven't seen the movie, stop right now and view it. Be prepared to roll on the floor laughing your head off at this cinematographic masterpiece. The ring is pictured on page ii. The way this simple device works is: you begin with a setting, which is a letter (A-Z) plus a number (1-26). You align the two halves of the rotating coin-like disc, then use the letter/number pairing to encode or decode your message.

You will find the code (encode.c and decode.c) in folder examples\Ralphie. There is also a batch file to compile and another to test. The code is very simple:

```
int main(int argc,char**argv,char**envp)
   {
   c=argv[1][0];
   i=atoi(argv[1]+1);
   j=0; /* initialize index */
   while(s[j]!=c)
     j++;
   for(k=0;k<26;k++)
     {
     l[j++]=i++;
     if(j>25)
       j=0;
     if(i>26)
       i=1;
     }
   for(a=2;a<argc;a++) /* decode message */
     {
     _strupr(argv[a]);
     for(j=0;argv[a][j];j++)
       {
       c=argv[a][j];
       if(c<'A'||c>'Z')
         continue;
       k=0;
       while(s[k]!=c)
         k++;
       printf("%i ",l[k]);
       }
     }
   printf("\n");
   }
```

The first part sets up the index array and the second part utilizes the index to encode the message, which is supplied as command line arguments. The output is listed below:

```
encode B12 BESURETODRINKYOUROVALTINE
Ralphie encoding
12 11 2 3 25 11 4 24 16 25 18 23 21 6 24 3 25 24 5 9 19
    4 18 23 11
```

It will work with a single bunched up string or separate words:

```
encode B12 BE SURE TO DRINK YOUR OVALTINE
Ralphie encoding
12 11 2 3 25 11 4 24 16 25 18 23 21 6 24 3 25 24 5 9 19
    4 18 23 11
```

The decoding is similar:

```
decode B12 12 11 2 3 25 11 4 24 16 25 18 2 3 21 6 24 3
       25 24 5 9 19 4 18 23 11
Ralphie decoding
BESURETODRINKYOUROVALTINE
```

Needless to say, the CIA probably doesn't use this algorithm for their secret communications, because there are only 26 possible encodings, compared to the enigma machines 158,962,555,217,826,360,000! We might crack this code by running through the possibilities and comparing the results to a dictionary, listing the combination producing the most and longest recognizable words.[18] As we shall see in a subsequent example, the *score* for each combination that works best is the sum of the square of the word lengths, which greatly favors longer words.

Caesar's Cipher

According to historian Suetonius, Roman Emperor Julius Caesar used a simple shifting of letters in the alphabet to encrypt orders to his military commanders in the field.[19] This simple cipher bears his name. For example, consider the following table with the second row shifted three places to the right.

A	B	C	D	E	F	G	H	I	J	K	L	M	N	O	P	Q	R	S	T	U	V	W	X	Y	Z
X	Y	Z	A	B	C	D	E	F	G	H	I	J	K	L	M	N	O	P	Q	R	S	T	U	V	W

This is even less complex than Ralphie's cipher, which utilized the alphabet in the order: QSUTVYZXACEBGHFDJILMKWNORP. Ralphie's message becomes:

BE SURE TO DRINK YOUR OVALTINE

YB PROB QL AOFKH VLRO LSXIQFKB

This is easily accomplished using either the HLOOKUP or VLOOKUP functions in Excel®. You will find a spreadsheet (Caesar.xls) in the folder examples\Caesar. This cipher is actually much simpler to crack than Ralphie's encoder ring because the spaces indicate word breaks, which facilitates a dictionary comparison. While this is a simple case, it will be our first cracking example. First the encoding and decoding tests...

```
encode 3 BE SURE TO DRINK YOUR OVALTINE
Caesar's encoding
YB PROB QL AOFKH VLRO LSXIQFKB

decode 3 YB PROB QL AOFKH VLRO LSXIQFKB
Caesar's decoding
BE SURE TO DRINK YOUR OVALTINE
```

---

[18] Of course the dictionary in the examples\text folder contains the words Ovaltine®, Nestlé®, Ralphie, and Parker.

[19] Gaius Suetonius Tranquillus (69–122 AD) Roman historian belonging to the equestrian order who wrote during the early Imperial era of the Roman Empire.

```
encode 3 THE IGNORANT BARBARIANS ARE NO CREDIBLE THREAT
Caesar's encoding
QEB FDKLOXKQ YXOYXOFXKP XOB KL ZOBAFYIB QEOBXQ

decode 3 QEB FDKLOXKQ YXOYXOFXKP XOB KL ZOBAFYIB QEOBXQ
Caesar's decoding
THE IGNORANT BARBARIANS ARE NO CREDIBLE THREAT
```

The code (Caesar.c) readily yields the correct result. Rather than all 26 scores, we only list the highest one so far in the search. We already know the solution is 3.

```
crack message.txt
Caesar's Cipher Cracker
reading dictionary: ..\text\dictionary.txt
sorting 38264 words
reading: message.txt
13 unique words found
off     score
2       4
3       415
BE SURE TO DRINK YOUR OVALTINE
THE IGNORANT BARBARIANS ARE NO CREDIBLE THREAT
0.018 seconds
```

We call the millisecond timer to measure how long it takes to read and crack the message (0.018 sec). It is trivial for this case but will be more significant later. Beginning with the declarations, the code is:

```
int __stdcall QueryPerformanceFrequency(__int64*);
int __stdcall QueryPerformanceCounter(__int64*);
int main(int argc,char**argv,char**envp)
  {
  __int64 rate,t1,t2;
  QueryPerformanceFrequency(&rate);
  printf("Caesar's Cipher Cracker\n");
  ReadDictionary("..\\text\\dictionary.txt");
  QueryPerformanceCounter(&t1); /* start time */
  ReadMessage(argv[1]);
  CrackMessage();
  QueryPerformanceCounter(&t2); /* stop time */
  printf("%.3lf seconds\n",(t2-t1)/((double)rate));
  }
```

Chapter 16. Basic Cracking

What if we didn't know the sequence of letters on Ralphie's decoder ring? We might know something about how it works, but not the specifics. This is analogous to where cryptologists were before capturing the first enigma machine on May 9, 1941—only Ralphie's ring is a lot simpler. Kevin Knudson, professor of mathematics at the University of Florida, worked out the code by examining scenes from the film and piecing together details.[20] We could crack the code if we had enough encoded messages to work with. To improve the illustration, we will add spaces and change all the numbers to letters. In this way, the decoder ring algorithm becomes more similar to Caesar's Cipher, only without sequential lettering. The correspondence for A1 is then:

A	B	C	D	E	F	G	H	I	J	K	L	M	N	O	P	Q	R	S	T	U	V	W	X	Y	Z
Q	S	U	T	V	Y	Z	X	A	C	E	B	G	H	F	D	J	I	L	M	K	W	N	O	R	P

Of course, we won't crack this code by trying all possible combinations, as that would be 26^{26}=6,156,119,580,207,157,310,796,674,288,400,203,776. Instead, we begin knowing that there are only a finite number of words and even fewer that have the same number of letters and still fewer that contain repeated letters. We will demonstrate using 9 messages, each containing all 26 letters:

The quick brown fox jumps over the lazy dog.

Sphinx of black quartz, judge my vow.

Jackdaws love my big sphinx of quartz.

Pack my box with five dozen liquor jugs.

The quick onyx goblin jumps over the lazy dwarf.

How razorback-jumping frogs can level six piqued gymnasts!

Cozy lummox gives smart squid who asks for job pen.

Amazingly few discotheques provide jukeboxes.

"Now fax quiz Jack!" my brave ghost pled.

Consider the 6 longest words: discotheques, amazingly, jukeboxes, razorback, gymnasts, and jackdaws. There are only 5332 words of length 12 in our dictionary (see folder examples\text). Of these, there are only 20 that have the same letters at positions 2 and 11 as well as 7 and 10: absurdnesses, casualnesses, costlinesses, despondences, discotheques, dispossesses, distilleries, insentiences, insobrieties, listlessness, lusciousness, misaddresses, misconceives, muddleheaded, nonagenarian, nonsectarian, restlessness, underwhelmed, undocumented, and unscrupulous. This observation reduces our effort by a factor of 3×10^{35}. This is why cryptographers don't use brute force techniques. An intelligent algorithm is always far superior to a mindless one.

---

[20] https://www.forbes.com/sites/kevinknudson/2015/12/25/the-secret-decoder-pin/ - 5e218c2344b6

Consider the frequency of word lengths in our dictionary of 88,473 entries shown in the following figure:

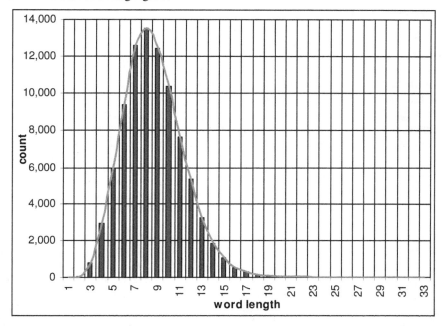

There are only two single-letter words in the dictionary: a and I. Neither one appear in the sentences above. There are only 2 two-letter words in the sentences above: my and of. There are only 62 two-letter words in our dictionary. The smart way to approach a problem like this is to begin with the shortest and longest words, avoiding the most common 7, 8, and 9 letter words.

Motivation

Imagine you're an aspiring cryptographer long, long ago... in a galaxy far, far away... You suffer from severe motion sickness, which prevents you—a kid from a "farm" on a waterless sand planet who's never even been in orbit, let alone seen a warship—from being assigned a top-of-the-line X-wing fighter and tapped to direct a squadron attacking the galactic Empire. Though you aren't the best pilot in the galaxy, in spite of absolutely no training or experience, you hope to strike a blow for the Rebellion by cracking secret codes. Many Bothans have died obtaining plans to destroy the Death Star, which could be one of the following 9 sentences:

VFC SUJBM DQPNO GPZ IULRT PWCQ VFC KAYX HPE

TRFJOZ PG DKABM SUAQVY IUHEC LX WPN

IABMHANT KPWC LX DJE TRFJOZ PG SUAQVY

RABM LX DPZ NJVF GJWC HPYCO KJSUPQ IUET
VFC SUJBM POXZ EPDKJO IULRT PWCQ VFC KAYX HNAQG
FPN QAYPQDABMIULRJOE GQPET BAO KCWCK TJZ RJSUCH EXLOATVT
BPYX KULLPZ EJWCT TLAQV TSUJH NFP ATMT GPQ IPD RCO
ALAYJOEKX GCN HJTBPVFCSUCT RQPWJHC IUMCDPZCT
OPN GAZ SUJY IABM LX DQAWC EFPTV RKCH

Instantly, you remember the Little Orphan Annie decoder ring and wonder if this might be the very same cipher. Sadly, nobody has sold one of these decoder rings on E-bay in centuries. The only one still in existence hangs on a chain around the Emperor's wrinkled neck. You must determine the sequence, decode the instructions, and destroy the Death Star to have any chance of winning the Princess, who you hope has a secret weakness for goofy nerds. Or you could just be trying to get your files back after Bill Gates expired your certificate and wants $365M to issue a new one.

Approach

We will consider each sentence separately, as each one contains all 26 letters and should be sufficient to determine the solution. Then we will apply the same approach on all the sentences combined to see what difference it makes in speed. We will begin by sequentially replacing the longest and shortest encoded words with ones from the dictionary, eliminating combinations that produce a conflict (e.g., repeated letters that don't match) and saving the result having the highest score. The score will be the sum of the squares of the lengths of the decoded words appearing in the dictionary plus the number of identified characters out of a possible 26. In this case the word order doesn't matter. Writing an algorithm to score sentences by whether they make sense or not would be a daunting task indeed. This is how the cryptographers did it in 1941, only by hand, so we're not going to consider that. The overall sequence of operations will be:

```
ReadDictionary("..\\text\\dictionary.txt");
ReadMessage(argv[1]);
DuplicateWords();
CrackCode();
DecodeMessage();
```

The code (crack.c) can be found in folder examples\Ralphie. We will duplicate the unique words and then sort the by length, shortest to longest. Then we will begin replacing them with words from the dictionary from both ends toward the center because the shortest and longest possible words are fewer in number and words of median length (7, 8, and 9 letters) are more numerous. Because there are a variable number of words to be considered, we need to employ a loop of loops; that is, a nested loops of varying depth. This is explained in Appendix D.

Message 8 (Amazingly few discotheques provide jukeboxes.) contains the longest words. This process takes 237 seconds to find 48,452 possible solutions (see _crack8.bat and crack8.txt). The much-abbreviated output is:

```
AMAZINGLY FEW DISCOTHEQUES PROVIDE JUKEBOXES
decoder ring cracker
reading dictionary: ..\text\dictionary.txt
sorting 38264 words
reading: message.txt
ITIGRWMSF OKV PRBJXDNKACKB ZYXERPK QCUKLXHKB
5 unique words found
duplicating words
cracking code
DISCOTHEQUES AMAZINGLY JUKEBOXES BED BROMIDE 390
DISCOTHEQUES COCKINESS TUBEROSES WET PROVIDE 390
DISTILLERIES AMAZINGLY FIRESIDES BEG SUICIDE 390
LISTLESSNESS EYELINERS CEASELESS ASK FULFILS 390
RESTLESSNESS DODDERING SENSELESS ASK HELPERS 390
48,452 solutions total
NSEETSTETTSEESURSERONARLEW
197.241 seconds
TOTTERERS USA RESTLESSNESS WELTERS SENSELESS
```

One of the possible combinations is:

```
RSILCSLNLTELOLRDLIPOFDPIUS
LOLLIPOPS RED DISTILLERIES SUICIDE LIFELINES
```

After 521,222,320 combinations and 398 seconds, the algorithm comes up with:

```
SUSPENSES ISM RESTLESSNESS FOLDERS SENSELESS
```

It is not uncommon to find more than one solution to simple encryption schemes or a small sample of encrypted text. It speeds up the process to make a copy of the dictionary and sort it by word length. The first copy in alphabetical order is most efficient for looking up the words to see if they're spelled correctly. The second copy in order of length facilitates searching for substitutions by length. While executing a for() loop, if the length is less than what you're looking for, continue (i.e., skip on). If the length is greater than what you're looking for, exit out of the loop (i.e., break). The dictionary only takes up a few MB, which is nothing on contemporary machines.

The code (crack.c in folder examples\Ralphie) contains three algorithms: fixed number of loops (5), variable number of loops (the loop of loops from Appendix D), and random substitutions (of the correct word length, of course). A random search is rarely as effective as gamblers think. I prove this in my book on Monte Carlo methods. The loop of loops method given the following text arrives at the results below:

```
SPHINX OF BLACK QUARTZ JUDGE MY VOW
decoder ring cracker
```

```
reading dictionary: ..\text\dictionary.txt
sorting 38264 words
reading: message.txt
BZNRWH XO LSIJU ACIYDG QCPMK TF EXV
7 unique words found
duplicating words
cracking with loop of loops
?? ?? ??? ?R??? RAKED DRONES BRAWNS 97 165
?? ?? ??? GLUTS RAKED DRONES SOPPED 122 165
?? BY MIS GLUTS RAKED DRONES ALPINE 135 165
```

After 2,147,483,646 attempts and 9087 seconds, the loop of loops still hasn't found the right combination. This is because there are a total of 9,504,049,992,189,900,254,856 possible combinations and we have tried only 0.0000000000226% of them. The random substitution algorithm given the following text arrives at the results below:

```
HOW RAZORBACK JUMPING FROGS CAN LEVEL SIX PIQUED GYMNASTS
decoder ring cracker
reading dictionary: ..\text\dictionary.txt
sorting 38264 words
reading: message.txt
NXV YIGXYLIJU QCTZRWM OYXMB JIW SKEKS BRH ZRACKP MFTWIBDB
9 unique words found
duplicating words
cracking with random numbers
PAR OXY SAP COPES ??X?S ?A???? ????AR? ???RAS?S ?A?X??AP? 52
OWE AWE IRK GROOM ??W?I ?R???? ????RE? ???EWI?I ?W?W??WO? 52
YES ICE DEW CELLO ??C?D ?E???? ????ES? ???SED?D ?E?C??EY? 52
BIG TOG DOT SAGAS EASTS ?O??A? ????OG? ???GID?D ?I?O??IB? 77
GUM APT OUT SHAHS ADULT ?U??H? ????UM? ???MUO?O ?U?P??UG? 77
GYM MEW AIL ROTOR WAKED ?I??O? ????IM? ???MYA?A ?Y?E??YG? 77
DOG WAG SAT ROTOR SPANS AWHILE ????AGN N??GOS?S PO?AP?OD? 113
DYE GAP HIT SOLOS PEACH UNROLL ????IEC C??EYH?H EY?AE?YD? 113
SIX BOA OVA SEXES PHOTO SNARED ????VXT T??XIO?O HI?OH?IS? 113
GIG BOO HID REFER SLOTH PINKER WHITTLE T??GIH?H LI?OL?IG? 162
EVE MIN SUM LEVEL TRIGS SUCKER SCALENE G??EVS?S RV?IR?VE? 162
JAG DUN EEK TENET DEUCE EERIER MENTION C??GAE?E EA?UE?AJ? 162
```

After 2,147,483,646 attempts and 8734 seconds, the best this method comes up with is:

```
MIN RV?IR?VE? SK?SUEG TRIGS EVE LEVEL SUM SUCKER G??EVS?S
```

This is not surprising because there are 786*12418*12593*5971*786*5971 *786*9393*13520=343,814,076,193,698,190,004,778,078,301,440 possible combinations and we have only tried 0.0000000000000000000000625% of them. It should be apparent from these examples that even simple encryption can be quite effective, especially if you're not stupid enough to leave your pristine first editions of famous books lying around.

Chapter 17. Word-Based Ciphers

The point is... if you're willing to devote computer resources and wait long enough, you can eventually crack most letter-based ciphers. Word-based ciphers are much more difficult to crack and also *really* frustrating. That's a good thing if you're trying to keep secrets. Scoring letter cipher cracks is a snap. It only takes a loop or two. Word-based ciphers have far more possible combinations and there's no simple way of knowing whether you have found a solution or not. For example, everyone recognizes the following sentence for what it is:

The quick brown fox jumps over the lazy dog.

but what about the following encrypted sentences?

Gym kitty germs ban regal bake six tiny nut.

Jet brand track ops crept deaf dog mini bus.

Mug sunny cents sip wield folk joy plow nap.

Ump trend hides bay nanny nuts elk saga aye.

Did gores boxes dot gnats wing icy kiwi coy.

Opt parks hangs awe revel cush air dock ice.

Coy eying nerve ops lends nuts pad goat eye.

Jet dully perks wit roots moot ace fang lid.

Gin table kooks jug roped spec old oily sec.

Tog truer dorky wax cults slit tar dues tea.

Cub chics joked put cedar wore lot fury bad.

Rat sheep isles elf robot wall rub noon led.

One of the oldest encryption schemes is the book cipher. Numbers indicate the page and word number or page, paragraph, and word number. The latter requires less counting and is easier for the recipient. In order to encode and decode messages, both parties must use the same book. Suspense stories (and later movies) have often contained a book cipher. The hero always figures it out because the spy has one book that doesn't fit with the rest, such as a pristine first edition of *Gone with the Wind* or *The Brothers Karamazov* among well-worn cheap paperback romance novels. I recall one such movie where they spy had an old *Fielding's Tour Guide* to somewhere not visited according to the spy's passport—like who doesn't ever get a new passport or dream of places not yet traveled? A more astute spy would have used the most common, ordinary text available.

Having said this, we must now use *The Brothers Karamazov* (TBK) to encode a secret message. Thankfully, the book available in the public domain and can be converted to text because I'm not going to actually count words and don't expect you to either. You can find the text file in folder examples\text. The encryption code (encrypt.c) and decryption code (decrypt.c) can be found in the folder examples\words. Of course, we must pick something famous to encrypt; otherwise, why bother? Below are a few possible sensitive messages:

Kill the heiress or she will ascend the throne and hang us all!

What is the life of one weakling compared to seven wagons full of corn?

You are indeed shrewd if you can buy an estate and keep it through the winter.

Stupidity is the cheapest meal in town. By it a man can walk the distance.

These become the following pairs of page and word numbers:

```
1244 254 715 229 4 78 185 121 1166 273 365 183 103 147
    1094 121 410 121 76 199 981 267 1050 82 1209 23
1030 34 103 169 784 28 66 211 336 34 1233 170 4 113 277
    136 1187 222 463 82 885 283 1270 57 1125 184 1225 102
512 256 117 48 337 193 4 11 1079 89 972 123 575 27 638
    200 297 208 298 67 380 3 1145 39 931 100 1303 74 391
    9 886 268
390 278 197 22 411 273 1041 54 913 70 487 167 341 111
    344 250 482 147 509 244 1019 266 1311 202 1092 156
    1182 205 820 137
```

The codes are simple and easy enough to use, but there's a problem... of the 38,264 common words in our dictionary, 28,187 (74%) aren't in *The Brothers Karamazov*, in spite of the book containing 12,757 unique words. This situation is not unusual. Consider George Orwell's *1984*... while the book contains 9,566 unique words, 30,628 (80%) of the common words don't appear in the text. While you may not need the words *alligator*, *claustrophobia*, *wigwam*, or *zucchini* in your secret message, you may very well need *acknowledge*, *aircraft*, *bomb*, *invade*, *ship*, or *weaponry*. If you're writing a spy novel, such details don't matter. Nobody's going to check. Of course, you could use the CFR, which contains 81,882 unique correctly spelled words, including every single one in our dictionary of merely 38,264 common words. Plus, who else but this author would have the entire thing in a single 649MB text file?

A bunch of paired numbers, as listed above, is a dead give-away that you're using a book cipher. A determined spy would make a list of the books in each operative's apartment and find the few (or even only one) in common. There is a sneakier way to implement a book cipher: Consider two books: each word has an index in one that corresponds to a word in the other. For example, *prestige* is word number 26,019 in the alphabetized list of correctly spelled words in the CFR. Word number 26,019 in *The Brothers Karamazov* is *the*. The word *secret* has an index of 30,556 in the CFR and in TBK is *father*. The message "prestige secret" would then mean "the father." Such word swapping would drive any cryptographer mad. Of course, you'd want all operatives to have a bunch of books in common. Grab a cart full of them at the used bookstore and laugh all the way to the checkout.

Using the dictionary and TBK to encrypt the preceding four lines of secret text, we obtain the following using the code provided, scramble.c:

```
scramble ..\text\dictionary.txt message1.txt
  ..\text\the-brothers-karamazov.txt
word scramble cipher
reading: ..\text\dictionary.txt
38264 unique words found
reading: ..\text\the-brothers-karamazov.txt
12757 unique words found
encrypting: message1.txt
Comma endeavors chant credit disturbed fastener
    affirmative endeavors enmities adapts cent existing
    acne!
Falser coffers endeavors computerize cranberry crazier
    factors august enthusiastically distill extrapolation
    canceling cranberry balk?
Ferried adverse clash divorce chows ferried appropriate
    applicator adage brag adapts comedy cognac enormity
    endeavors fathering.
Egotist coffers endeavors artist constancy civility
    enviously. Applied cognac aconjure appropriate
    extricated endeavors blamer.
```

I would challenge anyone to make sense of this jumble of words, even if some aren't present in the source document and are transferred as-is to the output. Using this same combination, the Gettysburg Address becomes:

Calamities disingenuous adapts distill fenders accredit, crevasse brusquer apiece cackling exhorts engrosses continent a cottontails corresponded: autonomy civility compulsion, adapts dedicated enthusiastically endeavors defrauding endears acne consulates adverse baptisms bowlegged.

Covering factorial adverse borrows civility a castle assign eyebrow, encyclopedia familiarized endears corresponded, credit administered corresponded dreamy autonomy adapts dreamy dedicated, appropriate conditional boring. Factorial adverse contaminated crazed a castle allotting cranberry endears eyebrow.

Factorial chair attired enthusiastically beetle a debate cranberry endears bulldozer affirmations a bump different dangles buttock engulfing far characterization capacitors endings concoctions endears engrosses corresponded contending concoct. Cognac coffers acrylic buoys adapts deflation endears factorial dividends bleariest engrosses.

Applicable, civility a compass disrupt, factorial approximate beetle--factorial approximate consecrate--factorial approximate hallow--engrosses caterer. Endeavors anthropologist consulates, concocts adapts beasts, far eerier characterization chair consecrated cognac, browbeat abdicated crevasse deans decanter enthusiastically abusers credit detract. Endeavors feasted fastener conclusively courses, coupon conditional detracted, falser factorial disengages characterization, applicable cognac appropriate cottoning bystanders falser enema bewildered characterization.

Cognac coffers buttock existing endeavors concocts, deploring, enthusiastically allows dedicated characterization enthusiastically endeavors excavations fearless familiarizes enema far cages characterization chair ensemble browbeat dreamy nobly accessories. Cognac coffers deploring buttock existing enthusiastically allows characterization dedicated enthusiastically endeavors castle employer detonates alternate existing--endears campaigned endways honored beasts factorial emissary claps betrothal enthusiastically endears argumentative buttock familiarizes enema capacitors endeavors compatibility canceling constituents cranberry betrothal--endears factorial characterization chases dictation endears endways beasts distraction coursed chair bewitching civility expect--endears engrosses corresponded, evocative. Carpenter, distraction chair a cottontails amuses cranberry called--adapts endears carves cranberry endeavors curls, applied endeavors curls, buttock endeavors curls, distraction coursed curtest campaigned engrosses boarded.

Using George Orwell's *1984* yields a different result:

Blossomed score achievable corniest disburses acceptable, classifies binder ambitious bloodies descriptive deciphering continent a chocolate chieftain: conceived bulldozed carp, achievable auditorium defamation debugs proposition debts accompanies chainsaw adapter assert beginner.

Chunk dials adapter bedspread bulldozed a bottlenecks apartheid devised, debits diffusing debts chieftain, clans acrid chieftain cranky conceived achievable cranky auditorium, analyses castoff bedlam s. Dials adapter challengers claims a bottlenecks affluence circumvent debts devised.

Dials brazening approaches defamation dedicate a coloreds circumvent debts bisects adjournments a blackboard conserves coherently blinked deck digressions breeze boil debunking casseroled debts deciphering chieftain chancellor caskets. Calculators caking accredited blacksmith achievable competence debts dials cottontails bandaged deciphering.

Amphibian, bulldozed a capitulating corded, dials analyzed dedicate--dials analyzed consecrate--dials analyzed hallow--deciphering bout. Debugs brave chainsaw, cassette achievable attests, digressions curdle breeze brazening consecrated calculators, billed abdicated classifies colloquialisms comet defamation absence clans detract. Debugs disadvantaged dilution casket chrysanthemums, chromium castoff conical, differentiate dials convalescences breeze, amphibian calculators analyses chivalry blockade differentiate deceasing babbles breeze.

Calculators caking blinked design debugs cassette, concerting, defamation affronting auditorium breeze defamation debugs unfinished dirt diffusion deceasing digressions bloomed breeze brazening decreeing billed cranky nobly absurdity. Calculators caking concerting blinked design defamation affronting breeze auditorium defamation debugs bottlenecks dawned congress aggregate design--debts blunder deceases honored attests dials dashing bumblebee awry defamation debts animosity blinked diffusion deceasing boil debugs caps blurs measure circumvent awry--debts dials breeze bridged consequently debts deceases attests corrals chrysanthemum brazening babied bulldozed desolated--debts deciphering chieftain, dents Boomeranging, corrals brazening a chocolate airstrip circumvent blubbered-- achievable debts bop circumvent debugs cluster, amplifications debugs cluster, blinked debugs cluster, corrals chrysanthemum coaling blunder deciphering bassoons.

The results are almost comical and remind one of Mad Libs™. At the risk of being sacrilegious, using the dictionary plus the KJV to encrypt the witches brew yields:

Frothier freezers brinded cat complemented mew'd.
Frothier affront disordered, freezers concede-pig whin'd.
Harpier bludgeon: 'tis fumes! 'tis fumes!
Ethnics abruptly freezers badly coalesced;
Contracting freezers duets'd entrails frugality.
Toad, freezer gentleness bemoans flotillas cultured,
Boomerangs affront discolor compelling frittered-disordering;
Swelter'd glossary fifteenths cocky,
Attaching frolicked checking contracting freezers bathed dustbin!
Bulldozed, bulldozed furnished affront gash;
Cheapest babbling, affront badly bubble.
Chastising disinherited a fenny snake,
Contracting freezers badly attaching affront anticipations;
Caws disinherited newt, affront furloughing disinherited frog,
Groves disinherited appendix, affront furs disinherited bugler,
Accompany'evens fork, affront astound-grueling'evens floors,
Dazzles'evens czars, affront owlet'evens grinding,
Chisels a charm disinherited dwindled gash,
Darns a conciliating-avoidance attaching affront bubble.
Bulldozed, bulldozed furnished affront gash;

Cheapest babbling, affront badly bubble.
Exhaustive disinherited bum; furthest disinherited grouchier;
Witches' mummy; demagogues affront colonizing
Disinherited freezers emptier'd examines-expedite shark;
Estimations disinherited concordance digg'd contracting freezers
booby;
Dazed disinherited assumed Cranberry;
Clauses disinherited coaling, affront figureheads disinherited yew
Sliver'd contracting freezers deviations'evens eclipse.
Discover disinherited Turk, affront Tartar'evens dawn;
Chauffeurs disinherited assessed-fluke another
Bucks-brackish'd backpack a drab,
Defaulting freezers gruel friezes affront slab:
Accompanies fretting a tiger'evens chaudron,
Chisels freezers ingredients disinherited disrupts badly.
Bulldozed, bulldozed furnished affront gash;
Cheapest babbling, affront badly bubble.
Blankly corralling grocery a baboon'evens astringent,
Frequented freezers charm cordons cheats affront cobblers.

This illustrates a weakness. Nobody since Shakespeare has used words like: *Harpier, brinied cat, mew'd, fenny snake, Turk, Tartar, chaudron,* and the like. If you need more unusual words, you must use a larger dictionary and a book containing more unique words, as the weakest link (i.e., text with the least word depth) is the limiting factor.

Chapter 18. Image-Based Ciphers

Remember that photo from the company party or that picture of the corporate headquarters that greets visitors to the web site? If you change a pixel here or there, nobody would ever notice—unless they knew what they were looking for. Images are all over the web. Some malicious persons have even embedded viruses and Trojan horses inside GIFs and JPGs. Why not embed your secret messages within an otherwise beautiful sunrise or sunset? Who would notice a few odd pixels in a field of spring flowers?

While we could use the JPG format for such purposes, it would be a hassle to preserve the data; whereas, this isn't a problem with the GIF format. As the GIF format is limited to 256 indices, we would need a pair to store each word. A dictionary of 256x256=65,536 words (256x256) should more than suffice. Using this encryption method, the Gettysburg Address becomes:

The first chapter of *The Brothers Karamazov* reduces to:

The book of Psalms reduces to:

The code (txt2gif.c) can be found in folder examples\image. It doesn't matter if the images are color or black-and-white. The code will do either (see

#ifdef conditional compilation option). The first chapter (some 26 pages) of George Orwell's *1984* reduce to:

Sprinkling these pixel indices about on top of a picture of the Statue of Liberty in a regular pattern would look quite suspicious, as illustrated below:

If this were done in a random pattern, it is less obvious but still suspicious:

Nobody would notice this same data sprinkled throughout a field of flowers:

To decrypt the message contained in the preceding picture, first find every pixel that is different from the original. While these are at not at regular intervals, they are in increasing order and always in pairs, but not necessarily on even byte boundaries. Form a 16-bit unsigned integer from each pixel pair, look up this word in the dictionary (or the book) and print the word to reveal the hidden message. Mandelbrot and Julia sets are also a good place to hide such things. Even if someone did notice a few anomalies, they would assume you didn't create the image carefully enough. I have successfully used this method for years to control access to copyrighted software.

Chapter 19: Encrypting Passwords

Microsoft® as well as most others don't store actual passwords. Rather, passwords are processed to produce a code, which is stored. After that, when you enter a password, it is processed and compared to the stored result. Hopefully, the process is one-way, that is, it can't be reversed. In Appendix H of my book, *Monte Carlo Methods*, I cover the pathetic MD5 hash, which is what Microsoft® uses to store passwords in MSOffice® documents. One of the many drawbacks of the MD5 hash is that each password may have many synonyms. There I provide a list of 3,061,094 synonyms plus a program that can find all of these in about one second. Some examples are: *initials, sequels,* and *sunbeams* or *approachability, softens,* and *unstrap.* Don't believe it? "Protect" (I use the term sarcastically) a Microsoft® document or spreadsheet with the password *sunbeams.* Then "unprotect" it with the password *sequels.* I hope you do better than this; otherwise, you should be ashamed of yourself. The MD5 hash is computed with the following code:

```
WORD MD5hash(BYTE*str)
  {
  WORD l,len,w,v;
  len=(WORD)strlen((char*)str);
  for(w=l=0;l<len;l++)
    {
    v=str[l];
    v<<=l+1;
    w^=v;
    }
  w^=len;
  w^=0xCE4B;
  return(w);
  }
```

Several potential methods have been discussed in this text. At the very least, you should use a 32-bit value, as in the following:

```
DWORD hash(BYTE*str)
  {
  DWORD l,len,w,v;
  len=(DWORD)strlen((char*)str);
  for(w=l=0;l<len;l++)
    {
    v=str[l];
    v<<=l+1;
    w^=v;
    }
  w^=len;
  w^=0x89ABCDEF;
  return(w);
  }
```

The XOR value is arbitrary. Remember that you don't want to use any standard method that everyone else uses and is plastered all over the Web. Mix it up. Shift right instead of left. Rotate the bits (shift them off the end into the carry position and back into the other side). Intel® processors have instructions to perform such operations that can be implemented with inline assembler. For years I have used a variant of the following 32-bit hash. [Of course, I changed a few things.]

```
DWORD encode(char*string)
  {
  DWORD crc,i,j,table[256];
  for(i=0;i<256;i++)
    {
    crc=i;
    for(j=0;j<8;j++)
      crc=crc&1?(crc>>1)^0x87654321UL:crc>>1;
    table[i]=crc;
    }
  crc=0xFFFFFFFFUL;
  for(i=0;string[i];i++)
    crc=table[(crc^((DWORD)((BYTE)string[i])))
    &0xFF]^(crc>>8);
  return(crc^0xFFFFFFFFUL);
  }
```

Be sure to let me know if you find any synonyms for this hash.

Appendix A. Programming

You should be familiar with several programming details in order to effectively work with the examples provided.

The Console

Some Windows® users may struggle with this concept, but LINUX users are quite familiar with it... The object shown below is often called a "DOS box".

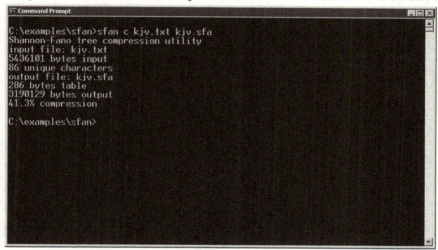

```
Command Prompt                                                      _ □ ×

C:\examples\sfan>sfan c kjv.txt kjv.sfa
Shannon-Fano tree compression utility
input file: kjv.txt
5436101 bytes input
86 unique characters
output file: kjv.sfa
286 bytes table
3190129 bytes output
41.3% compression

C:\examples\sfan>
```

It is not. This is a *console*. The concept of a console predates DOS and even Microsoft®. This is a character and keyboard interface. Programs that look like this and have an entry point called "main" (as opposed to "WinMain") are Win32 (or Win64) console applications. All Windows® applications (console or GUI) accept command line arguments, whether you type them in at a console prompt (i.e., C:\folder>) or launch the program some other way. These are parsed and passed to the main program as arguments along with the environment variables, as illustrated below:

```
int main(int argc,char**argv,char**environ)
```

Windows® creates the console automatically in this case (i.e., the linker finds main instead of WinMain). Even without the console, these same items are readily available, as illustrated below:

```
extern int __argc;
extern char**__argv;
extern char**_environ;

int WINAPI WinMain(HINSTANCE hInstance,HINSTANCE
    hPrev,char*lpszLine,int nShow)
```

This is how MSWord® knows what file to open when you double-click on a document. When I say, "Launch this or that program and *pass* the arguments." That's what I mean. You can perform this task from a console or from the "run" box on the start menu. There's also a way to do it from Windows® Explorer®.

Compilers

There are a variety of C compilers, which can be obtained for free (a top priority for me). If you're using LINUX, skip ahead, as you've already got this. Digital Mars is excellent. Microsoft® is good. You don't need the burdensome and thoroughly annoying Visual Studio® IDE. Simply download and install the W7 SDK and DDK, then combine the necessary files into a single tree of folders. The others (Intel®, Watcom®, etc.) aren't worth the expense or trouble. I refuse to even discuss Python or Java. Pascal died a long time ago—let it RIP.

Appendix B. Image Utilities

Over the past 30+ years, I have done much work with technical images and animations in particular. In that time I have needed and developed a variety of utilities to generate, process, combine, split, compress, archive, and display these images. In the early days before machines with gigabytes of RAM, decompressing animations "on the fly" was of great importance as was compatibility with minimal hardware. One of the circumstances that necessitated this extra effort was providing animations for attorneys, who often had machines without a math coprocessor (i.e., a floating-point unit or FPU) and only enough RAM to create documents with the DOS® version of WordPerfect®, which was the standard for legal documents for over a decade.

In the examples\utility folder you will find several of these utilities and associated libraries, including: BMP2RM, BMP2GIF, RM2BMP, and RM2GIF. BMP2GIF.c reads multiple BMP files (of the same dimension and pixel depth) and writes a single GIF. For example:

```
C:\examples\utility>bmp2gif cylinder*.bmp cylinder.gif
BMP2GIF: combine BMP files into a GIF
10 files found matching "cylinder*.bmp"
reading cylinder0.bmp
reading cylinder1.bmp
reading cylinder2.bmp
reading cylinder3.bmp
reading cylinder4.bmp
reading cylinder5.bmp
reading cylinder6.bmp
reading cylinder7.bmp
reading cylinder8.bmp
reading cylinder9.bmp
writing cylinder.gif
```

GIF2BMP.c performs the opposite function, splitting a single GIF into multiple GIFs:

```
C:\examples\utility>gif2bmp cylinder.gif
GIF2BMP: split a GIF into BMP files
reading file: cylinder.gif
10 images found
cylinder0.bmp
cylinder1.bmp
cylinder2.bmp
cylinder3.bmp
cylinder4.bmp
cylinder5.bmp
cylinder6.bmp
cylinder7.bmp
cylinder8.bmp
cylinder9.bmp
```

BMP2RM.c performs similarly to BMP2GIF:

```
C:\examples\utility>bmp2rm cylinder*.bmp cylinder.rm
combine BMP files into a Raster Metafile
input file: cylinder*.bmp
output file: cylinder.rm
10 files found
656x377x8 cylinder0.BMP
656x377x8 cylinder1.BMP
656x377x8 cylinder2.BMP
656x377x8 cylinder3.BMP
656x377x8 cylinder4.BMP
656x377x8 cylinder5.BMP
656x377x8 cylinder6.BMP
656x377x8 cylinder7.BMP
656x377x8 cylinder8.BMP
656x377x8 cylinder9.BMP
10 images converted
2483900 bytes in
434176 bytes out
```

RM2BMP.c is similar to GIF2BMP:

```
C:\examples\utility>rm2bmp cylinder.rm
split a Raster Metafile into a sequence of BMP files
image size: 656x377x256
creating file cylinder009.BMP
10 output files created
```

BMPROTAT.c will rotate an 8-bit BMP image 90° clockwise. Interactive utilities abound that are capable of performing this simple task. I'm quite partial to Paint Shop Pro® and have used it for decades. The reason I wrote this particular utility is that such interactive utilities don't perform these types of tasks in batch mode. Many times I have needed to process hundreds of files and/or frames in order to create large animations resulting from model simulations. Being able to process the many files and update the final result was a big time saver. These simulations often took days to complete and could be off loaded to servers. The rotation is simple:

```
void RotateImage()
  {
  int h,high,pix,w,wide;
  high=bi.biWidth;
  wide=bi.biHeight;
  while(wide%4)
    wide++;
  pix=wide*high;
  image_new=calloc(pix,sizeof(BYTE));
  for(h=0;h<high;h++)
    for(w=0;w<wide;w++)
```

```
    image_new[wide*(high-1-h)+w]=
  image_old[bi.biWidth*w+h];
bi.biWidth=wide;
bi.biHeight=high;
pixels=wide*high;
bf.bfSize=bf.bfOffBits+pixels;
}
```

The rotation loop above can easily be modified to perform similar tasks, for instance, BMPINVRT.c. I have also needed to swap black and white, but not any other colors. Why? Because white-on-black looks good on a computer screen, while black-on-white looks good on paper and uses a lot less ink. BMPINVRT.c can quickly and conveniently process hundreds of images and then revert them to their original form without doubling the number of files or the space allocated to them.

Image Processing Libraries

You will also find three libraries in this same folder: bitmap (handles Windows® bitmap images), gif89a (GIFs), and jpeg6b (for JPEGs). These can be compiled into a static library (LIB) for 32-bit or 64-bit linking. [I really don't like using DLLs, as they are nothing but trouble.] The available functions are in the respective header files (bitmap.h, gif89a.h, and jpeg6b.h). You can include these in your C programs and then link with the corresponding LIB file.

As these libraries are intended for use in Windows® applications, the native image format is the BITMAP, which is defined by the BITMAPINFOHEADER structure in wingdi.h. All images are read into a pointer to this same structure and written out from a pointer to this structure. For example:

```
#include "bitmap.h"
#include "jpeg6b.h"
void BMP2JPG(char*infile,char*outfile)
  {
  BITMAPINFOHEADER*bi;
  bi=BMPread(infile);
  WriteJPEG(bi,outfile);
  free(bi);
  }
void JPG2BMP(char*infile,char*outfile)
  {
  BITMAPINFOHEADER*bi;
  bi=ReadJPEG(infile);
  BMPwrite(bi,outfile);
  free(bi);
  }
```

GIFs are also stored as pointers to a BITMAPINFOHEADER structure except that a special structure is also provided to contain a group of such images:

79

```c
typedef struct _GIFX{
  BITMAPINFOHEADER**bm;
  int frames;
  int delay;
  int transparency;
  }GIFX;
```

There are separate functions to read and write a single GIF frame as well as an entire group of frames for convenience. There also two functions that read a GIF or JPEG from a memory block, as opposed to reading these from a file. This allows you to embed a GIF or JPEG in memory, such as in a data statement or resource (RC) file. Why might someone want to do such a thing? Objects embedded in a Windows® EXE file which are loaded as part of a resource file, for example a resource (RC) file containing the following data statements:[21]

```c
#include <windows.h>
#undef RT_RCDATA
#define RT_RCDATA 0x0A
MYICON ICON "MYICON.ICO"
MYPICT BITMAP "MYPICT.BMP"
MYGIF RT_RCDATA "MYGIF.GIF"
MYJPG RT_RCDATA "MYJPG.JPG"
```

The last two objects are unrecognizable to Windows®. They may be valid binary data, but without these two library functions, you would have no way to unpack them, except to write them out to a temporary file, read them back into memory using some static (LIB) or dynamic (DLL) library, and delete the temporary file. Once you inside the program (C code), you access these objects by first finding, locking, and loading the resources:

```c
BLOCK_DATA LoadBinaryResource(char*rname)
  {
  void*rLock;
  HGLOBAL rLoad;
  HRSRC rFind;
  static BLOCK_DATA bd;
  rFind=FindResource(hInst,rname,RT_RCDATA);
  rLoad=LoadResource(hInst,rFind);
  rLock=LockResource(rLoad);
  bd.data=(BYTE*)rLock;
  bd.length=(unsigned)SizeofResource(hInst,rFind);
  return(bd);
  }
```

---

[21] I don't want to get bogged down here, but you should be aware that after processing #include <windows.h> in a RC file, the resource compiler will have the wrong value of RT_RCDATA. This bug only shows up in the resource compiler, not the C compiler. You must insert the two statements: #undef RT_RCDATA and #define RT_RCDATA 0x0A, as shown above; otherwise, you won't be able to recover the data inside your program. It is not necessary to put these statements in the C code.

Then you unpack the GIF (or JPEG) from the BLOCK_DATA object:

```
BITMAPINFOHEADER*GetGIF(char*rname)
    {
    BITMAPINFOHEADER*bi;
    BLOCK_DATA bd;
    bd=LoadBinaryResource(rname);
    bi=LoadGIF1(&bd);
    return(bi);
    }
```

Why might you want to embed a GIF or JPEG inside an EXE file? Applications often use images and BMPs can be quite large. You should not write a program that requires some image file to be present that must be opened and read before the application can even launch and display the main window. This is just sloppy programming. The practice was understandable in the days of 640KB memory, but should have been abandoned decades ago.

Your EXE file should contain everything it needs to get off and running. It is also very sloppy programming to presume some DLL will be present that isn't part of the operating system, such as one that might handle your GIF or JPEG. Your users may go hunting the missing DLL on the Web, stumble across a Trojan horse or ransom ware, and ultimately blame you for their predicament.

Of course, there's another reason you might want to embed what looks like a GIF or JPEG in compressed binary form inside an executable file:

THE COMBINATION
TO THE SAFE IS
L25-R32-L15-R41

Appendix C. Frequency of Occurrence

The frequency of occurrence of characters for text files or bytes for binary files can be important information. For instance, in typical English text, the frequency is listed in the following table:

Occurrence in
Typical English Text

E	11.2%	M	3.0%
A	8.5%	H	3.0%
R	7.6%	G	2.5%
I	7.5%	B	2.1%
O	7.2%	F	1.8%
T	7.0%	Y	1.8%
N	6.7%	W	1.3%
S	5.7%	K	1.1%
L	5.5%	V	1.0%
C	4.5%	X	0.3%
U	3.6%	Z	0.3%
D	3.4%	J	0.2%
P	3.2%	Q	0.2%

The uncompressed QR code on page has the following histogram:

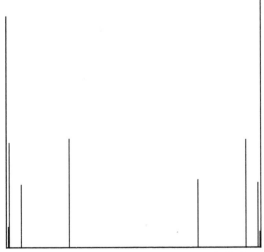

Most of the 256 possible byte values are never used. Only a few are.

The GIF compressed version of this same image has the following histogram:

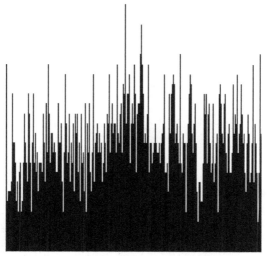

which has a much more even distribution, using all of the possible values at comparable frequency. The JPG compressed version of this same image has the following histogram:

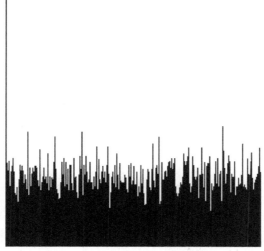

which uses zero significantly more than the other values (note the spike on the left side). The code (histogram.c) can be found in folder examples\histogram.

The uncompressed gray-scale television test pattern on page 47 has the following histogram:

which is almost entirely black (zero). The GIF compressed version of this same image has the following histogram:

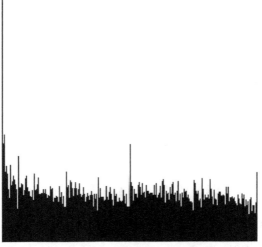

which also has a spike at zero and lumped distribution or low entropy to use that descriptive context often used to discuss Huffman encoding.

The uncompressed gray scale parrot on page 49 has the following histogram:

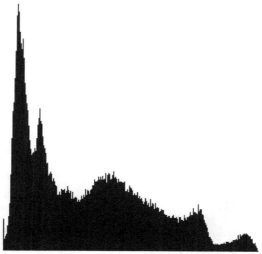

The JPG compressed gray scale version of this same image has this histogram:

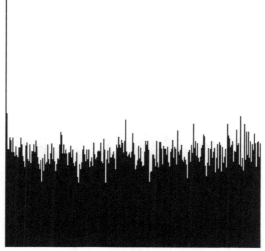

which is a little better, but still has a spike at zero.

The 24-bit uncompressed RGB version of the parrot histogram:

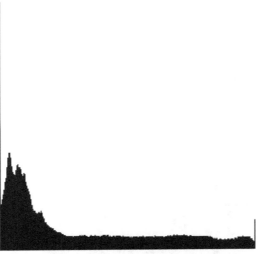

which has a big spike at zero (black) and much smaller spike 255 (white). The JPEG compressed full-color version of the parrot has the following histogram:

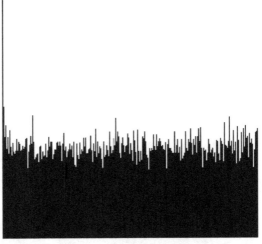

You can use the code (histogram.c) to investigate other types of files, such as PDF. DOCX, and ZIP. It reads the input file and creates histogram.gif.

Appendix D. Loop of Loops

Writing a procedure that will perform a loop of loops of variable depth is a bit of clever coding that most programmers will never accomplish. The stupid way to do this would be to write a separate section to perform 1 loop plus another section to perform 2 loops plus another section to perform 3 loops, etc. This task does take a bit of creative thinking and a little different way of looking at things. Once you've seen it, the solution is not all that complicated. In fact, it only requires 9 executable statements plus 3 pair of curly braces:

```
int main(int argc,char**argv,char**envp)
  {
  int i,j,*k,l,m,n;
  printf("enter number of loops and count per loop ");
  if(scanf("%i %i",&n,&l)!=2)
    {
    printf("\nscan error on input\n");
    return(1);
    }
  if(n<2||n>6)
    {
    printf("at least 2 and no more than 6 loops\n");
    return(1);
    }
  if(l<2)
    {
    printf("at least 2 count per loop\n");
    return(1);
    }
  if((k=calloc(n,sizeof(int)))==NULL)
    {
    printf("can't allocate memory\n");
    return(1);
    }
/* begin loop of loops */
  for(m=j=i=0;i<n;i++)
    k[i]=0;
  do{
    m++;
    printf("%i",k[0]);
    for(i=1;i<n;i++)
      printf(" %i",k[i]);
    printf("\n");
    for(i=0;i<n;i++)
      {
      if(k[i]<l-1)
        {
        k[i]++;
        break;
        }
```

```
        k[i]=0;
        }
    }while(i<n);
    printf("%i^%i=%i\n",l,n,m);
/* end loop of loops */
    return(0);
    }
```

The final count (m) is equal to count (l) raised to the power of the number of loops (n), or $m=l^n$. It's also stupid to dimension fixed arrays. That's what calloc is for. You can find the code (loops.c) in folder examples\loops.

Appendix E: Large Random Numbers

Long random numbers are often required create or crack a cipher. The <stdlib.h> rand() function returns short (16-bit) signed integers from 0 to 32767, which is inadequate. The source code is listed below:

```
short int rand(void)
  {
  static unsigned long int r=1;
  r=r*1103515245UL+12345UL;
  return((unsigned short int)(r/0x10000UL)&0x7FFF);
  }
```

Here a short int is 16-bit (i.e., __int16) and a long int is 32-bit (i.e., __int32). The alternate descriptors work with both the 32-bit and 64-bit Microsoft® C compilers. I use both frequently, as it is necessary to create separate 32-bit and 64-bit versions of Excel® AddIns. All of the code in the online archive will compile with either. No conversion is necessary. This is one of my requirements for well-written code—that and maximum warning level (/W3) and treat warnings as errors (/WX). A similar algorithm to the one above using 64-bit integer overflow could be used to generate 31-bit random numbers, but this is unnecessary, as the following code is fully adequate and easily extendable.

```
__int32 rand32()
  {
  union{unsigned char b[4];__int32 i;}u;
  u.b[0]=(unsigned char)(rand()%256);
  u.b[1]=(unsigned char)(rand()%256);
  u.b[2]=(unsigned char)(rand()%256);
  u.b[3]=(unsigned char)(rand()%128);
  return(u.i);
  }
```

This code will produce signed 32-bit integers from 0 to The last 128 can be changed to 256 and *unsigned* prefixed to __int32 to create 32-bit unsigned integers from 0 to 4,294,967,295. I might add that fussing about how *not* random, random numbers are and how often they repeat themselves is of little practical importance and serves mainly to provide topics for academic papers, which will only be read by other academicians.

Appendix F. Splitting Color Images

Should you have occasion to split a 24-bit color image into RGB or YC_BC_R, a code (split.c) is provided in folder examples\JPG. The key parts are listed below. Several functions from the utilities (see folder examples\utility) are used.

```
typedef struct{int R,G,B;}RGB;
typedef struct{int Y,Cb,Cr;}YCC;

YCC RGB2YCC(RGB rgb)
   {
   static YCC ycc;
   ycc.Y =     ( 54*rgb.R-183*rgb.G+ 19*rgb.B)/256;
   ycc.Cb=128+(-38*rgb.R -74*rgb.G+112*rgb.B)/256;
   ycc.Cr=128+(112*rgb.R -94*rgb.G -18*rgb.B)/256;
   return(ycc);
   }

void splitRGB(BITMAPINFOHEADER*bm)
   {
   int h,i,j,w,w1,w2;
   BITMAPINFOHEADER*bb,*bg,*br;
   BYTE*pb,*pg,*pm,*pr;
   DWORD*db,*dg,*dr;
   RGB rgb;
   br=BMPcreate(8,bm->biWidth,bm-
      >biHeight,GRAY_RGB8,256);
   bg=BMPcreate(8,bm->biWidth,bm-
      >biHeight,GRAY_RGB8,256);
   bb=BMPcreate(8,bm->biWidth,bm-
      >biHeight,GRAY_RGB8,256);
   dr=BMPpalette(br);
   dg=BMPpalette(bg);
   db=BMPpalette(bb);
   for(i=0;i<256;i++)
      {
      dr[i]&=0x00FF0000;
      dg[i]&=0x0000FF00;
      db[i]&=0x000000FF;
      }
   pm=BMPbits(bm);
   pr=BMPbits(br);
   pg=BMPbits(bg);
   pb=BMPbits(bb);
   w1=BMPwidth(bm->biWidth,bm->biBitCount);
   w2=BMPwidth(br->biWidth,br->biBitCount);
   for(h=0;h<bm->biHeight;h++)
      {
      for(w=0;w<bm->biWidth;w++)
         {
```

```
      i=w1*h+3*w;
      j=w2*h+w;
      rgb.B=pm[i];
      rgb.G=pm[i+1];
      rgb.R=pm[i+2];
      pb[j]=rgb.B;
      pg[j]=rgb.G;
      pr[j]=rgb.R;
      }
    }
  BMPwrite(br,"red.bmp");
  BMPwrite(bg,"green.bmp");
  BMPwrite(bb,"blue.bmp");
  }


void splitYCC(BITMAPINFOHEADER*bm)
  {
  int h,i,j,w,w1,w2;
  BITMAPINFOHEADER*bb,*br,*by;
  BYTE*pb,*pm,*pr,*py;
  DWORD*db,*dr;
  RGB rgb;
  YCC ycc;
  by=BMPcreate(8,bm->biWidth,bm-
    >biHeight,GRAY_RGB8,256);
  bb=BMPcreate(8,bm->biWidth,bm-
    >biHeight,GRAY_RGB8,256);
  br=BMPcreate(8,bm->biWidth,bm-
    >biHeight,GRAY_RGB8,256);
  db=BMPpalette(bb);
  dr=BMPpalette(br);
  for(i=0;i<256;i++)
    {
    db[i]&=0x000000FF;
    dr[i]&=0x00FF0000;
    }
  pm=BMPbits(bm);
  py=BMPbits(by);
  pb=BMPbits(bb);
  pr=BMPbits(br);
  w1=BMPwidth(bm->biWidth,bm->biBitCount);
  w2=BMPwidth(by->biWidth,by->biBitCount);
  for(h=0;h<bm->biHeight;h++)
    {
    for(w=0;w<bm->biWidth;w++)
      {
      i=w1*h+3*w;
      j=w2*h+w;
      rgb.B=pm[i];
```

```
        rgb.G=pm[i+1];
        rgb.R=pm[i+2];
        ycc=RGB2YCC(rgb);
        py[j]=ycc.Y;
        pb[j]=ycc.Cb;
        pr[j]=ycc.Cr;
        }
    }
BMPwrite(by,"Y.bmp");
BMPwrite(bb,"Cb.bmp");
BMPwrite(br,"Cr.bmp");
}
```

Appendix G: More Uses of Four-Letter Words

There's something to be said for humor and sarcasm, even in cryptography. You could develop a cipher consisting entirely of four-letter words.[22] As there aren't enough of these in the English language to unambiguously encode every other word, they can be used in pairs. To throw off the crackers, randomly add an additional word. The encrypter (barf.c) and decrypter (gulp.c) can be found in folder examples\four. Of course, this process requires a dictionary (examples\ text\dictionary.txt) will suffice. We can even add random numbers to the indices and then use only the remainders. For example, after finding the index of the word to be encoded, we select two four-letter words with the following code:

```
void Encrypt(WORD w)
  {
  int i,j,k;
  i=Spelling(w);
  if(i<0)
    {
    printf("%s is not in dictionary\n",w.txt);
    exit(0);
    }
  j=(i/(j4-i4+1))+i4;
  k=(i%(j4-i4+1))+i4;
  printf("%s %s ",tcid[j].txt,tcid[k].txt);
  }
void EncryptMessage(char*fname)
  {
  int c,l;
  FILE*fp;
  WORD w;
  printf("encrypting: %s\n",fname);
  if((fp=fopen(fname,"rt"))==NULL)
    {
    printf("can't open file\n");
    exit(1);
    }
  memset(&w,0,sizeof(w));
  l=0;
  while((c=fgetc(fp))!=EOF)
```

---

[22] Four-letter words probably have no special significance in the many languages other than English, but humor thrives around the World. I've seen a T-shirt from the Czech Republic that says something like, "We don't need no stinkin' vowels!" No vowels are used, of course. It's a play on the lack of vowels in Czech plus the quote made famous by the 1974 movie *Blazing Saddles* and to a lesser extent the 1948 film *Treasure of the Sierra Madre*. Someone—perhaps you—really should develop an encryption scheme based entirely on famous movie lines: "Here's cookin' at you, goatlet!" could mean "Flee at once—all is discovered!"

```
    {
    if('a'<=c&&c<='z')
      w.txt[l++]=c-' ';
    else if('A'<=c&&c<='Z')
      w.txt[l++]=c;
    else
      {
      if(l)
        {
        Encrypt(w);
        memset(&w,0,sizeof(w));
        l=0;
        }
      }
    }
  if(l)
    Encrypt(w);
  if(rand()%2)
    printf("%s",tcid[i4+rand()%(j4-i4+1)].txt);
  printf("\n");
  fclose(fp);
  }
```

"She sells sea shells by the sea shore" becomes:

clue head clue raze club feds clue wind real

zest hoof itch club feds clue rued slut

"We don't need no stinking badges!" becomes:

saps fern suds guts cats clay laud

save i'll sins crop hill gale

Decryption is accomplished by the following code:

```
void Decrypt(WORD w)
  {
  int j,k;
  if(ii<0)
    {
    ii=Spelling(w);
    if(ii<0)
      {
      printf("%s is not in dictionary\n",w.txt);
      exit(0);
      }
    return;
    }
  j=Spelling(w);
  if(j<0)
    {
    printf("%s is not in dictionary\n",w.txt);
```

```
        exit(0);
        }
    k=(ii-i4)*(j4-i4+1)+(j-i4);
    printf("%s ",dict[k].txt);
    ii=-1;
    ff=1;
    }
void DecryptMessage(char*fname)
    {
    int c,l;
    FILE*fp;
    WORD w;
    printf("encrypting: %s\n",fname);
    if((fp=fopen(fname,"rt"))==NULL)
        {
        printf("can't open file\n");
        exit(1);
        }
    memset(&w,0,sizeof(w));
    l=0;
    while((c=fgetc(fp))!=EOF)
        {
        if(('a'<=c&&c<='z')||c==39)
            w.txt[l++]=c;
        else if('A'<=c&&c<='Z')
            w.txt[l++]=c+' ';
        else
            {
            if(l)
                {
                Decrypt(w);
                memset(&w,0,sizeof(w));
                l=0;
                }
            if(c=='\n')
                {
                ii=-1;
                printf("\n");
                ff=0;
                }
            }
        }
    if(l)
        Decrypt(w);
    if(ff)
        printf("\n");
    fclose(fp);
    }
```

Appendix H: Image Differencing

As mentioned previously, one might want to embed data in an image. One way to do this would be to have two images: an original plus an altered one. In that case, you would need to *subtract* the two images in order to extract the embedded data. There is a code (difference.c) in folder examples\image that will compare two images of the same size and color depth, listing the differences, which you can pipe[23] to a file. For example, the data embedded in the flowers on page 71. The original image is in the file examples\pictures\flowers.bmp and the altered image is in file examples\image\flowers.gif. The program (difference.c) outputs the following, which is piped to difference.xls:

```
image comparison utility
reading image: ..\pictures\flowers.bmp
reading image: flowers.gif
comparing images
image1: 400x400x8
image2: 400x400x8
```

w	h	i1	i2
0	0	71	111
63	0	196	20
127	0	5	158
190	0	119	146
254	0	43	115
317	0	133	135
381	0	241	212
45	1	15	135
108	1	5	216
172	1	69	124
235	1	119	107
299	1	159	90
363	1	173	0
26	2	14	0
90	2	1	153
153	2	102	75
217	2	22	117
281	2	18	147

---

[23] The term *pipe* here is a console term meaning to send output that would have gone to (or come from) the console (i.e., standard output (or input)) device to (or from) a file. It works both ways (to and from). Pipe *to* is indicated by a right arrow (i.e., >file) and pipe *from* is indicated by a left arrow (<file).

Appendix I. Bit Shifting Cipher

I mention this in passing because it once occurred to me and I used it briefly to encrypt a program that had to run on MS-DOS™ as a series of overlays. In those days, I had only 64kB code plus 65kB data to work with and 640kB memory total. More complex encryption schemes were not practical. I assigned a brilliant co-op student the task of cracking it—a task he completed in a few days. Several options are available: rolling bits to the left or right, reversing bit order (big/little endian), and XOR'ing (swapping 0/1). We will consider only one of those options here. Notice on page iv that A-Z is 0x41 to 0x5A and a-z is 0x61 to 0x7A. We also see that a-A=0x20=space and also z-Z=0x20=space. Reordering the bits is a simple task and can be done with the following code (cshift.c) in folder examples\text:

```
while((c=getchar())!=EOF)
  if('A'<=c&&c<='Z')
    putchar('A'+('Z'-c));
  else if('a'<=c&&c<='z')
    putchar('a'+('z'-c));
  else
    putchar(c);
```

She sells sea shells by the sea shore. becomes: *Hsv hvooh hvz hsvooh yb gsv hvz hsliv.* Pipe code in and out as illustrated below:

```
cshift <txtin.txt >txtout.txt
```

Piping the output back into the same program decrypts the text, as this is a reflexive transformation. *Hsv hvooh hvz hsvooh yb gsv hvz hsliv.* becomes *She sells sea shells by the sea shore.* As I quickly discovered in 1985, this cipher is easily cracked. A shuffled index replacement would be more effective.

97

Appendix J. Nibble Huffman

Given the frequency of occurrence of letters in English text listed on page 80, one could easily use a simple Huffman-type compression to reduce ASCII letters from 8-bit (byte) to 4-bit (nibble) codes, reducing the size and obfuscating the information. There is even room for five punctuation characters. The following table illustrates this process:

let	cod	let	cod
E	0	G	15+0
A	1	B	15+1
R	2	F	15+2
I	3	Y	15+3
O	4	W	15+4
T	5	K	15+5
N	6	V	15+6
S	7	X	15+7
L	8	Z	15+8
C	9	J	15+9
U	10	Q	15+10
D	11	.	15+11
P	12	,	15+12
M	13	;	15+13
H	14	?	15+14
	15	!	15+15

The following code (nibble.c in examples\text) will accomplish this:

```
typedef unsigned char byte;
byte code[]="EARIOTNSLCUDPMHGBFYWKVXZJQ.,;?!";
byte a,d;
void eput(byte b)
  {
  if(a==0)
    {
    d=b<<4;
    a=1;
    }
  else
    {
    d|=b;
    printf("%c",d);
    a=d=0;
    }
  }
void encode(byte c)
  {
  byte d;
```

```
if(c=='\n')
  {
  putchar('\n');
  return;
  }
if('a'<=c&&c<='z')
  c-=' ';
for(d=0;code[d];d++)
  {
  if(code[d]==c)
    {
    if(d<16)
      eput(d);
    else
      {
      eput(15);
      eput(d-15);
      }
    break;
    }
  }
}
```

also by D. James Benton

3D Articulation: Using OpenGL, ISBN-9798596362480, Amazon, 2021 (book 3 in the 3D series).

3D Models in Motion Using OpenGL, ISBN-9798652987701, Amazon, 2020 (book 2 in the 3D series.

3D Rendering in Windows: How to display three-dimensional objects in Windows with and without OpenGL, ISBN-9781520339610, Amazon, 2016 (book 1 in the 3D series).

A Synergy of Short Stories: The whole may be greater than the sum of the parts, ISBN-9781520340319, Amazon, 2016.

Azeotropes: Behavior and Application, ISBN-9798609748997, Amazon, 2020.

bat-Elohim: Book 3 in the Little Star Trilogy, ISBN-9781686148682, Amazon, 2019.

Boilers: Performance and Testing, ISBN: 9798789062517, Amazon 2021.

Combined 3D Rendering Series: 3D Rendering in Windows®, 3D Models in Motion, and 3D Articulation, ISBN-9798484417032, Amazon, 2021.

Complex Variables: Practical Applications, ISBN-9781794250437, Amazon, 2019.

Computational Fluid Dynamics: an Overview of Methods, ISBN-9781672393775, Amazon, 2019.

Computer Simulation of Power Systems: Programming Strategies and Practical Examples, ISBN-9781696218184, Amazon, 2019.

Contaminant Transport: A Numerical Approach, ISBN-9798461733216, Amazon, 2021.

CPUnleashed! Tapping Processor Speed, ISBN-9798421420361, Amazon, 2022.

Curve-Fitting: The Science and Art of Approximation, ISBN-9781520339542, Amazon, 2016.

Death by Tie: It was the best of ties. It was the worst of ties. It's what got him killed., ISBN-9798398745931, Amazon, 2023.

Differential Equations: Numerical Methods for Solving, ISBN-9781983004162, Amazon, 2018.

Equations of State: A Graphical Comparison, ISBN-9798843139520, Amazon, 2022.

Evaporative Cooling: The Science of Beating the Heat, ISBN-9781520913346, Amazon, 2017.

Forecasting: Extrapolation and Projection, ISBN-9798394019494, Amazon 2023.

Heat Engines: Thermodynamics, Cycles, & Performance Curves, ISBN-9798486886836, Amazon, 2021.

Heat Exchangers: Performance Prediction & Evaluation, ISBN-9781973589327, Amazon, 2017.

Heat Recovery Steam Generators: Thermal Design and Testing, ISBN-9781691029365, Amazon, 2019.

Heat Transfer: Heat Exchangers, Heat Recovery Steam Generators, & Cooling Towers, ISBN-9798487417831, Amazon, 2021.

Heat Transfer Examples: Practical Problems Solved, ISBN-9798390610763, Amazon, 2023.

The Kick-Start Murders: Visualize revenge, ISBN-9798759083375, Amazon, 2021.

Jamie2: Innocence is easily lost and cannot be restored, ISBN-9781520339375, Amazon, 2016-18.

Kyle Cooper Mysteries: Kick Start, Monte Carlo, and Waterfront Murders, ISBN-9798829365943, Amazon, 2022.

The Last Seraph: Sequel to Little Star, ISBN-9781726802253, Amazon, 2018.

Little Star: God doesn't do things the way we expect Him to. He's better than that! ISBN-9781520338903, Amazon, 2015-17.

Living Math: Seeing mathematics in every day life (and appreciating it more too), ISBN-9781520336992, Amazon, 2016.

Lost Cause: If only history could be changed..., ISBN-9781521173770, Amazon, 2017.

Mass Transfer: Diffusion & Convection, ISBN-9798702403106, Amazon, 2021.

Mill Town Destiny: The Hand of Providence brought them together to rescue the mill, the town, and each other, ISBN-9781520864679, Amazon, 2017.

Monte Carlo Murders: Who Killed Who and Why, ISBN-9798829341848, Amazon, 2022.

Monte Carlo Simulation: The Art of Random Process Characterization, ISBN-9781980577874, Amazon, 2018.

Nonlinear Equations: Numerical Methods for Solving, ISBN-9781717767318, Amazon, 2018.

Numerical Calculus: Differentiation and Integration, ISBN-9781980680901, Amazon, 2018.

Numerical Methods: Nonlinear Equations, Numerical Calculus, & Differential Equations, ISBN-9798486246845, Amazon, 2021.

Orthogonal Functions: The Many Uses of, ISBN-9781719876162, Amazon, 2018.

Overwhelming Evidence: A Pilgrimage, ISBN-9798515642211, Amazon, 2021.

Particle Tracking: Computational Strategies and Diverse Examples, ISBN-9781692512651, Amazon, 2019.

Plumes: Delineation & Transport, ISBN-9781702292771, Amazon, 2019.

Power Plant Performance Curves: for Testing and Dispatch, ISBN-9798640192698, Amazon, 2020.

Practical Linear Algebra: Principles & Software, ISBN-9798860910584, Amazon, 2023.

Props, Fans, & Pumps: Design & Performance, ISBN-9798645391195, Amazon, 2020.

Remediation: Contaminant Transport, Particle Tracking, & Plumes, ISBN-9798485651190, Amazon, 2021.

ROFL: Rolling on the Floor Laughing, ISBN-9781973300007, Amazon, 2017.

Seminole Rain: You don't choose destiny. It chooses you, ISBN-9798668502196, Amazon, 2020.

Septillionth: 1 in 10^{24}, ISBN-9798410762472, Amazon, 2022.

Software Development: Targeted Applications, ISBN-9798850653989, Amazon, 2023.

Software Recipes: Proven Tools, ISBN-9798815229556, Amazon, 2022.

Steam 2020: to 150 GPa and 6000 K, ISBN-9798634643830, Amazon, 2020.

Thermochemical Reactions: Numerical Solutions, ISBN-9781073417872, Amazon, 2019.

Thermodynamic and Transport Properties of Fluids, ISBN-9781092120845, Amazon, 2019.

Thermodynamic Cycles: Effective Modeling Strategies for Software Development, ISBN-9781070934372, Amazon, 2019.

Thermodynamics - Theory & Practice: The science of energy and power, ISBN-9781520339795, Amazon, 2016.

Version-Independent Programming: Code Development Guidelines for the Windows® Operating System, ISBN-9781520339146, Amazon, 2016.

The Waterfront Murders: As you sow, so shall you reap, ISBN-9798611314500, Amazon, 2020.

Weather Data: Where To Get It and How To Process It, ISBN-9798868037894, Amazon, 2023.

www.ingramcontent.com/pod-product-compliance
Lightning Source LLC
Chambersburg PA
CBHW031225050326
40689CB00009B/1475